WHAT DO YOU STAND FOR?

Stories About Principles That Matter

EDITED WITH COMMENTARY BY

Jim Lichtman

D0566906

Published by Scribbler's Ink
Printed in Canada

ISBN 0-9648591-1-4

Library of Congress Control Number: 2004092437

Jacket and book design by Frank Goad

October 2004

For JIM GAMBLE and DAVE SHELDON

The wise man does not teach by words but by deeds.
–LAO TZU, 6th century Chinese philosopher

contents

it began like this...

I WAS SPEAKING TO A GROUP of about four hundred managers, administrators and trustees in Philadelphia – a group that was genuinely interested in ethics. Not an easy sell, ethics. But since this group handled large amounts of teacher pension funds, they felt more than a little sense of duty.

At the end of the talk, I left them with a story told to me by my ethics professor, Michael Josephson. "Imagine," I told them, "you have a difficult decision to make at work. If you do the right thing, serious consequences, you might lose your job. If you do the *wrong* thing, you may get a promotion or a bonus out of it! Now, imagine that you've made your decision and you take it home to your family. There are two ways this story could end.

"First way: You sit your family down and say, 'I did something at work today that I'm not very proud of, but I want you to know that I did it because I love you and I want to take care of you.'

"Second way: 'I did something at work today that concerns me and may have serious consequences that would affect us all. We might have to move out of this nice home. I might have to pull you out of school. I may lose my job. I just want you to know that I did what I thought was the right thing. And I love you and I hope you'll support my decision.'

"Which of the two versions would you rather tell your family?" The room was silent.

The intent was to leave them with the question that if we all had to make decisions with our family looking over our shoulder, would we be comfortable, proud even, of the decisions we make?

In line to check out of the hotel, luggage in hand, an ever-so-polite, gray-haired man touches my arm, "…excuse me, I want to thank you for your talk this morning. I just wanted you to know," he continued, "that story you told about 'taking it to your family,' that actually happened to me."

I stepped out of line and put my bag down. It was one of those moments where, in spite of the commotion and noise of a large hotel lobby, I heard nothing else but this man's story.

"It was the '30s," he began, "the depths of the Depression, and my father did not have regular work, but he had a reputation for being a man of great integrity. One day, the owner of a local bar asked him to come to work as his bartender. It seems the man was having trouble finding someone who was honest and could keep his hands out of the till. Knowing my father to be rigorously honest, the man offered him thirty-five dollars a week if he took the job. However, there was one problem: my father did not drink; both he and my mother came from families who were opposed to drinking on religious principle. Interested in any offer that could help his family financially, my father was troubled because his principles did not hold with working in a bar. So, he came home and brought the decision to his family.

"He sat us all down, my mother, older brother, and myself

and told us about the offer. He explained that, although this was a good opportunity to make a lot of money, it would mean doing something that he was morally opposed to. "'So, I'm asking you,' my father said, 'what should I do?'

"My brother, who was eight at the time and two years older than me, asked, 'Will Grandpa know about this job?'

"'No,' my father said. 'Grandpa lives several hundred miles away, in the next state.'

"Then my brother asked, 'Will *God* know about this?'

"My father smiled, realizing what he'd believed all along, and said that he wouldn't be taking that job."

Whether you agree or disagree that drinking is immoral is not the point. This man saw, by his father's own actions, that it was more important to stand by his principles than achieve personal gain, even with a family to support.

Looking into the man's 70-something eyes, I could see that this still had a powerful effect on him. "I was six-years-old at the time," he said, "but I never forgot that moment. Whenever I had a tough decision to make, I always remembered what my father said and what it meant – that his integrity was more important than anything else."

I thanked him for his story. We smiled, shook hands and I left. The whole moment lasted maybe four minutes, but it was all I thought about for the next ninety minutes on the train.

It didn't take long to realize that there were more stories like this, stories that could inspire us to a higher standard of conduct. If we are ever to bring about meaningful change in our world, surely we must start with ourselves. So, I came up with a question, sent it out to athletes, CEOs, clerics, journalists, political leaders, students, teachers, and others, then collected their responses.

The result is this book, whose purpose is to encourage each of us to live up to our highest aspirations.

1

the examined life

SOMETIMES THE PURPOSE OF A QUESTION is to learn something about ourselves. And sometimes that question comes in the form of a painting.

It was on the second floor of New York's Metropolitan Museum of Art that I was first transformed by a painting. I've always been drawn to representational art that tells a story, and this one told an intriguing one.

An old man sits on a bed, stripped to the waist, talking to a group of friends. His hand is outstretched, reaching for a drink. But something is strange.

This isn't a drinking party. The people around him clearly do not look like they are enjoying themselves. And the location is dark, surrounded by stone walls, as if they are in a cellar or prison.

What's going on here?

The gallery label reads: *The Death of Socrates*. Closer study reveals that all of the great philosopher's friends and colleagues are in various stages of agitation, shock, grief; even the man handing Socrates the cup seems to be doing so more out of a forced sense of duty than anything else; but what seemed strangest of all was Socrates, himself. He's sitting upright, proud even, resolutely making one, final philosophic point while reaching for the cup of poisonous hemlock.

Socrates had been condemned to death by a jury of Athenian citizens. But why was a philosopher being put to death? What had this man possibly have done? Lie? Steal? Kill some important official?

Socrates' crime was questioning the status quo.

During much of the 4th and 3rd centuries BC, Athens was arguably the center of philosophical thought in the Greek-speaking world, and Socrates – through his greatest disciple Plato – was known perhaps as the wisest, believing that "the only good is knowledge and the only evil is ignorance." However, Socrates also believed that "true knowledge exists in knowing that you know nothing," but, "...in *knowing* that you know nothing, that makes you the smartest of all."

Sounds like an episode of *Seinfeld*, doesn't it?

Socrates' life was a quest for wisdom, specifically knowledge of what he referred to as "the good." Socrates believed that "to *know* the good is to *do* the good." He believed that ethical truth was absolute and understandable, much like the truths of mathematics; that if we taught these truths, people would then "...do the good." At the time, people believed that what was popular was also right. So, the great sage questioned people to see if what was popular also made sense. That's when he took his particular brand of Q&A to the streets – to poets, carpenters, soldiers, politicians, citizens of all kinds. But after questioning these people, Socrates discovered they weren't all that wise.

Now Socrates never hurt anybody; he just aggravated the hell out of them by causing them to think. A little bit of thinking, not bad; a lot of thinking – especially about things like which gods people should worship and how they should conduct their lives – *too* bad…for Socrates.

So, in 399 BC, according to Plato, Socrates was placed on trial for "not believing in the gods the state believes in and introducing different new divine powers, and also for corrupting the young." There were no lawyers or judges in those days. Individuals brought suits against other individuals, who then had to defend themselves. Athenians seem to have been an especially litigious lot. Schools of rhetoric did big business because citizens had to be trained to defend themselves in court.

The jury for the trial was a staggering 500. The size of the jury shows how much free time upper class Athenians had. Imagine the lunch break chaos!

Speaking in his own defense, Socrates said, "I do nothing but go about persuading you all, old and young alike, not to take thought for your persons or your properties, but and chiefly to care about the greatest improvement of the soul. I tell you that virtue is not given by money, but that *from* virtue comes money and every other good of man, public as well as private. This is my teaching, and if this is the doctrine which corrupts the youth I am a mischievous person."

Not exactly *Matlock*, is he?

But here's the surprise – the vote was closer than even Socrates would have guessed: 280 to convict, 220, opposed. Unfortunately, close only counts in horseshoes, so Socrates was sentenced to death by lethal drink.

By this time, however, many citizens had second thoughts. Embarrassed that they had condemned to death their most prominent citizen, a group of Athenians conspired to bribe Socrates' prison guard and allow him to escape. But Socrates reasoned that such an act would violate the law.

In drinking the hemlock with one hand while making a philosophical point with the other, Socrates affirmed two things: his obligation as an Athenian to submit to Athenian justice even if that "justice" was in error; and his conviction for truth over what was popular. "...as long as I draw breath...I shall not cease to practice philosophy,...to point out to anyone...whom I happen to meet: Good Sir, you are an Athenian, a citizen of the greatest city with the greatest reputation for both wisdom and power; are you not ashamed of your eagerness to possess as much wealth, reputation and honors as possible, while you do not care for nor give thought to wisdom or truth?"

When Socrates said, "The unexamined life is not worth living," he was telling us that only through self-examination can we improve. Each of us is faced with ethical choices: choices involving loyalty, respect, compassion, honesty, fairness, duty; choices that constantly test who we are and what we stand for. It is not enough to say, "Honesty is the best policy;" we have to demonstrate that in our lives. It is not enough to believe that compassion is good for the soul without practicing a compassionate nature.

By questioning others about their beliefs, by challenging their principles, Socrates was telling us that the philosophy was meant as a way of living.

"Not life," Socrates said, "but a *good* life, is to be chiefly valued."

2

the right thing

WE KNOW WE CAN FIND STORIES of people who do it wrong, but where can we find stories of people who do it *right*?

The challenge was to find stories that would demonstrate principles in action, how real people faced real problems and made real decisions. But I needed a question compelling enough to stimulate a response. Looking through my first book, *The Lone Ranger's Code of the West*, the second sentence jumped out at me: What do we stand for? A good start, but it needed something more. Eventually, I came up with this:

- What do you stand for – what principle(s) have you lived by?
- Describe a 'moment of principle' in which your convictions were tested or a story in which you were inspired by another.

Some people responded with stories, others without. Some preferred an interview; others referred me to a speech or a personal account from a book; all reflected a variety of backgrounds, values and beliefs that we could read and find ourselves.

These first responses illustrate a diversity of principles that matter as well as focus on a common rule known to us all.

STEVE ALLEN wrote 52 books, acted on stage, films, and TV, created and hosted *The Tonight Show* as well as more than 1,000 episodes of *Steve Allen Shows,* and in his spare time, composed more than 9,000 songs! In the last several years of his life, he traveled around the country speaking to groups about the importance of ethics and morality. Although I received a couple of letters from him, I wish I had had an opportunity to meet and speak with the man, who was not only one of the wittiest and most intelligent people on the planet but one of the most sincere and direct in his beliefs about what he stood for.

> I wish I had a fascinating, perhaps even unique answer to your question as to what principles I have lived by. Unfortunately I don't. The principles that seem important to me are simply those that have been serviceable for the human race for unknown thousands of years. It is better to tell the truth than to lie. It is better to do no harm to others – and in fact to substantially help them – than to attack them. It is better to be honest in business dealings than dishonest.

After Allen's death, Jayne Meadows Allen, award-winning actress of Broadway, film, and TV, submitted this story about one of many principled stands taken by her husband.

> It was well after one o'clock in the morning. Steve and I had just returned home from an enormous Hollywood party when the phone rang. It was Marlon Brando who said he had to talk to Steve immediately and asked if I had

Shirley MacLaine's phone number.

The two men spoke briefly and I heard Steve repeat, "That's LAX, United, eight o'clock, I'll be there. Oh, no problem, Jayne will call Shirley right now."

"About what?" I asked.

"Marlon wants Shirley to fly to Sacramento with us today to help convince Governor Brown to stay the execution of Caryl Chessman."

"Chessman, the rapist?" I reminded Steve.

"Please, just call Shirley."

Several hours later, the three activists were on their way to Sacramento. The next day, every major newspaper in the United States carried a front-page picture of the three superstars at the California state capitol.

They were crucified by the conservative press. Steve's sponsors, as well as his employers at NBC, were up in arms. Marlon and Shirley were movie stars without the pressures from advertising agencies and networks.

I warned Steve, "Darling, my parents were missionaries who devoted their lives to fighting evil, but you are in the public eye, and all your courageous (and very public) fighting of organized crime, the atomic bomb, and now this stand against the death penalty will affect your television ratings."

Steve answered, "I care much more about the ratings of mankind than about the ratings of my TV show."

And so he did, and that's one of the main reasons I married him. He was a principled gentleman, like my father.

IN THE EARLY 1940s, Norman Corwin was nearly as well known

as Franklin Delano Roosevelt and much admired. "His brilliant dramas, fantasies, and documentaries reached into American homes – and across an ocean – as far as the radio could carry his words." Author Ray Bradbury calls Corwin, "...the greatest director, the greatest writer and the greatest producer in the history of radio."

However, it wasn't *just* that Norman Corwin was exceptional in his versatility as writer, director, and producer; what made his work inspiring was that it could reach beyond a simple box in a room and command your attention. He could get you to imagine, feel, and, more importantly, think. *We Hold These Truths* was written to be a celebration of The Bill of Rights, but airing just eight days after the Japanese bombing of Pearl Harbor, it became a timely reminder of what the country stands for. Given the events of September 11th, 2001, I listened to it again and was moved.

Among enduring universal precepts, including the Ten Commandments and similar ethical prescriptions both religious and secular, there is one that I think outranks all others. It is the Golden Rule, expressed most famously by Jesus (Matthew 7:12) but proposed earlier in the credos of Plato, Confucius, and thinkers of less glamorous report.

Abundant lip service is given the concept of doing unto others as we'd have done to ourselves, but no prescription is ignored more widely. To begin with, the Golden Rule is positive, whereas most active moral principles are negative. Of the Commandments, for example, eight of the Ten are thou-shalt-nots.

Think of the effect, if the principle of Doing Unto Others were fully practiced across all boards. There would be neither theft nor murder; kindness, courtesy and the whole family of related benignities would flourish; racial and other discrimination would disappear; the homeless would find shelter; war would wither because so few would subscribe to its practice and upkeep.

The Rule is a principle I strive to honor. Mostly I succeed, but on occasions when I lapse, I am troubled and contrite until and unless I set things right.

CHARLES LEWIS founded the Center for Public Integrity after eleven years as an investigative reporter at ABC News and CBS News, most recently as a producer for *60 Minutes*. The Center is a nonpartisan, nonprofit organization based in Washington, D.C. that examines public service and ethics-related issues. The Center has published over 200 investigative reports, and Lewis has been the author of several of them, including *The Cheating of America* and *The Buying of the President*.

From childhood, there has been one pretty simple principle by which I have tried to live. It is the Golden Rule. To me, it all boils down to that.

When a politician lies or steals, when the powers that be of a corporation, a labor union, a church, or a hospital are avaricious and duplicitous, violating the public trust or worse, the public health and welfare, the Golden Rule has been ignored. When affluent communities dump their toxic waste in a poor area, or disproportionately pollute the environment with little or no accountability, the

Golden Rule has been ignored. When civil or human rights are violated or harmful products are knowingly kept on the market, the Golden Rule has been ignored.

I have had many "moments of principle," as you can imagine, operating a nonprofit, nonpartisan watchdog organization in Washington. I have had donors attempt to stifle our investigative findings (they failed). I have had powerful corporations attempt to bully us with legal threats into changing our findings (they failed). I have had powerful politicians threaten to embarrass us with public criticism if we don't look elsewhere (it didn't work). I have had hate group militias threaten us because of our findings (nothing happened). And all of this is just in the last decade.

Once, back in 1978 or so, when I was 25 years old, I was an off-air investigative reporter for ABC News in Washington. We were deep into an investigation of a troubled federal agency, and I had found some original, circumstantial evidence suggesting possible corruption by a top government official. Specifically, this gentleman had become a millionaire, acquiring more than 30 houses in Alexandria, Virginia in just three or four years. I had spent hours studying dusty grantor-grantee records of real estate transactions, after receiving a "tip." How could a public official have possibly done this? Had he received some cash from government contractors doing business with his agency?

My bosses at the network, in Washington and New York, were thrilled with this information. They wanted to film the homes, with the dollar amounts splashed across the screen, and promote the segment very heavily on the network evening news program. This exuberance was coming down from on high.

I balked and killed my own story. After the initial discovery, I had spoken to the gentleman's banker, his realtor, and ultimately, the public figure himself. The man and his wife both had advanced degrees from prestigious universities and personal hobbies of buying rundown homes in dubious areas for $30,000 or $40,000, renovating them, and selling them for $100,000 or more. I determined that it was possible to have achieved such wealth, legally and properly.

My bosses were furious – and there were intense arguments. I was seen as a pain-in-the-ass, self-righteous, professionally naïve or worse, stupid, an inexperienced pup. Nonetheless, I flatly refused to participate any further or allow my name to be on the story in any way.

A week later, a well known, Pulitzer Prize-winning investigative journalist – a competitor to us – exposed the potential enrichment of this official. The FBI launched an investigation, which lasted for two years. The man and his wife were humiliated and demoralized, and they literally moved away to New England. Ultimately, the FBI reached the same conclusion I had and no charges were ever filed.

A dramatic "gotcha" story, laden with qualifiers and caveats, could have been written and aired, based upon what we had. But it would have been disingenuous and a cheap shot.

I did the right thing, and my news organization was not a party to ruining a man's reputation. But I was in the doghouse for a few weeks for my inconvenient stubbornness.

ONE OF THE THINGS THAT I ENJOY about reading Carolyn Hax is that she doesn't allow a lot of "stuff" to get in the way of dealing with the sticky situations in life. Hax writes an advice column for the "under-30 crowd," with the suitably smart title, *Tell Me About It*. And she does! But her real secret is this – she doesn't take herself (or anyone else, for that matter) too seriously. Her response has a way of reminding us about the importance the "small things" play in our lives.

As principles go, the Golden Rule is remarkably efficient. Clear, concise, covers everything. I've found that it draws a straight line to integrity, as well as providing the only civil approach to doing unto others.

I do have a moment that I recall often, not one of inspiration so much as clarity. I grew up on a busy suburban street with few stop signs, no lights, not much of a shoulder, and zero deterrents to speed, so when someone stood in the middle of it, it was something you noticed. I must have been a teenager, a young one maybe, when I saw my father out there. He had his old dirt shovel and was scraping up the awfulness that was the latest critter to be denied the other side. I'm sure I'd seen Pops do this before – the smell usually showed up before the town did, and the houses were close to the street – but this time, my mom was watching, too. "Do you realize," she said, "that he's the only one who'll get out there and do that? He's the only *man*."

With one image and two sentences I learned that "man" – and as I would later come to understand, "woman" or simply "adult" – meant the person who saw what the common good demanded, and did it. Didn't wait for some other sap to do it, didn't wait to be asked, didn't pay an underling, didn't whine, didn't procrastinate. Did it.

As attitudes go, it seems like it's born to greatness: to go off to war! To give that raise to charity! To rescue the damsel from the oncoming train! But I find it comes to me most in smallness. Put dirty clothes in the hamper, resist the urge to beat the red light, get a job and pay the bills, lag behind to leave more on the table when a companion under tips. With all of these things, "left undone" means "inflicted on somebody else," and what kind of person is comfortable with that? Not a mature one. Another thing I learned that day, in retrospect: What a difference a dad makes.

A CONVERSATION WITH DR. FREDDYE DAVY of Hampton University's Honors College in Virginia led her to use my questionnaire in an essay contest for Hampton's annual President's Award. All thirty-two submissions expressed an uncommon level of candor and commitment to a higher standard. Three expressed a special appeal for service to a purpose beyond their own ambitions.

The first comes from Courtney Thompson who is currently attending Purdue University where she is earning a master's degree in American Studies. What struck me most about her essay was her reflective look at the Golden Rule. When I asked her what stood out about her essay after re-reading, she confided, "Why didn't it dawn on me sooner?"

"Do unto others as you would have them to do unto you." These words have echoed in my mind since early childhood. Through the years, I have made serious attempts to follow the Golden Rule, endeavoring to set the pendulum of reciprocity in motion and striving to maintain its constant movement. Continuously, I struggled to extend a mutual kindness to others, usually commensurate with the kindness that I received. I always believed that I understood the full import of these words, until recently.

In December, I visited Mombassa, Kenya, a country rich in land, culture, and tradition. The roads were filled with vendors, consumers, workers in transit, tourists, the poor, and the homeless. The first days, Hashim, the friend that I traveled to visit, gave willingly to many suffering from severe conditions of destitution and utter helplessness, often exchanging larger bills for easy-to-dispense change. After observing his daily routine of selflessly giving, I reflected upon the ideal symbolized in the counsel "do unto others as you would have them to do unto you." Before I could censor my thoughts, inwardly I questioned, "But what about when others are unable to do unto you?" The answer came as Hashim's willingness to give continued over the course of the remaining weeks. "You must give to the world *more* than the world gives to you." Indeed, this was the real essence represented by the Golden Rule.

In that experience, I learned more than I had in a lifetime about the gift of giving. I have since accepted and faithfully practiced the true application of this principle in my life with one modification. Though the change is a single word, the difference is profound. I have resolved that for the rest of my life, not only will I do unto others; I will do unto others *unconditionally*.

Dᴵᴄᴋ Cᴀᴘᴇɴ's ᴄᴀʀᴇᴇʀ is a unique blend of newspaper publishing and diplomacy. After leaving as publisher and chairman of The Miami Herald, Capen served as the United States Ambassador to Spain and Assistant Secretary of Defense. Known for his commitment to personal values and a positive approach to life, he is a nationally recognized columnist, author, and speaker on contemporary trends in America.

Capen offered the following "Check List" from his book, *Finish Strong: Living Your Faith in The Secular World & Inspiring Others in the Process*.

THE HIGHER GROUND CHECK LIST

- Anchor your life to higher ground. Simply do the right thing.
- Live your life according to this higher calling – God's calling.
- Don't always look to others to set the moral example because some won't. Only you can determine the key personal values that should guide your life.

- Demand that your leaders set an example. That's what leadership is all about.
- Conduct your life in an exemplary manner. If you can be a positive influence on just one person each day, you will make an enormous contribution.
- Center your life on principle not popularity. Today's hero can be tomorrow's bum.
- When you make mistakes, admit to them, apologize, and learn from the experience. Others may be willing to forgive you, but don't forget that you must accept the consequences of your actions.
- Build trusting relationships, starting with your family and friends. Trust counts, big time.
- Don't put yourself in positions where anyone could even think that you are doing something wrong. Perceptions are as powerful as reality.
- Cherish your family, close friends and marriage. Each is key to a meaningful life.
- Be an encourager, especially to those without hope.
- Always be optimistic, even when you think our country is falling apart. We have a long history of improving from one generation to the next. Soon it will be your turn.
- Serve others. The spirit of volunteerism is key to our future.

DR. MICHAEL DeBAKEY is a respected physician and surgeon whose pioneering work in the field of cardiovascular surgery has earned him international recognition. He is credited with inventing and perfecting scores of medical devices, techniques, and procedures, which have led to healthy hearts and productive lives for millions throughout the world. Additionally, he is credited with developing the Mobile Army Surgical Hospitals – M.A.S.H. Units – for the military.

Dr. DeBakey has earned an enviable reputation as a medical statesman. His writings are reflected in more than 1,600 published medical articles, chapters, and books on various aspects of surgery, medicine, health, medical research, and medical education, as well as ethical, socio-economic, and philosophic discussion in these fields. He led the movement to establish the National Library of Medicine, which is now the world's largest and most prestigious repository of medical archives.

In 1969, he received the highest honor a United States citizen can receive, the Presidential Medal of Freedom with Distinction.

The principles I live by are the ones my parents instilled in me from my earliest remembered years.

By word and example, they taught me that the honor of my family name and a close family bond were more precious than anything, including wealth; that honesty, integrity, and trustworthiness will always stand the test of time; that kindness, compassion, altruism, patriotism, and public service lift the heart and nourish the soul; that self-discipline, industry, and determination can overcome almost all obstacles; and that the pursuit of excellence is not only fulfilling, but exhilarating. They showed me, by their own charitable deeds, that it is, indeed, more blessed to give than to receive, and they insisted that everyone can, and should, make some contribution to humanity, no matter how small. It was, in fact, their model of humanitarianism and our exemplary family physician who sparked my early desire of becoming a physician.

My parents' principle of patriotism tested me when I was a young academic physician, on the threshold of my long-held dream of a career in medical research, teaching, and patient care. I had a number of research subjects that intrigued me and propelled me to spend long hours in the laboratory searching for answers to the causes and cures of several unsolved disabling and fatal diseases. Then America became involved in World War II. To enter the military at this stage meant interrupting my fervent desire to probe the deep chasms of medical mysteries – to surrender some of the most productive years of my carefully charted course.

But the love of my country and its principles of freedom and personal responsibility that my parents taught me pulled me in the direction of signing up for service. Then I was declared an "essential" member of the faculty at Tulane Medical School in New Orleans. I could stay in my post guilt-free and pursue the career that I had longed for since earliest childhood. I discussed my situation with my parents, who urged me to make my own decision, but who reminded me of every citizen's responsibility. I knew what I must do: I asked the School to release me from the "essential" category and joined the U.S. Army. At the end of the War, I was asked to delay my return to civilian status and remain yet another year in the Surgeon General's Office to help organize the transfer and care of wounded servicemen to hospitals in this country. I readily agreed, and at the end of that period returned to Tulane Medical School and resumed a most fulfilling and enjoyable career there and, later, at Baylor College of Medicine in medical research, teaching, and patient care. I have never regretted allowing altruism to supersede self-interest by extirpating those fertile years from my academic career, and I was able, through good fortune, to pursue research and scholarly activities while I was in the service.

JIM NIXON has worked in the aviation industry for more than thirty years. Nixon's story talks about the influential effect a popular radio and TV character had on his own "rules for living."

The answer to your question is going to sound a little corny, but it happens to be true.

As a boy, I rebelled against authority of any kind. Discipline inspired outright hostility. I hated organized activity. I loathed team sports. I harassed my teachers. So I certainly wasn't going to listen to my parents. They made the mistake of thinking that plunking me down in Sunday school would surely accomplish a good portion of my grounding in the Christian ethic, just as it was for the offspring of other young adult friends of theirs who were raising families after World War II. So every week I was dutifully shuffled off to Sunday school classes for ninety minutes while they attended services upstairs. For me, it proved to be an hour and a half of hell.

What a rebellious kid like me with a fertile imagination might have done to mess up his life is anyone's guess. But one particular evening about this time, my father thought my brother and I might enjoy a kid's western program, which came on at 6:30 p.m., just as my mom was washing up the supper dishes. One episode of *The Lone Ranger* and I was hooked. The character of the mysterious Ranger embodied all that was good and honorable. He righted wrongs, helped those in need, and never stayed around to be thanked. Those young people listening to the program were constantly exposed to the Ranger's Creed – rules for living – which we could apply to our own growing up.

The Ranger never got me back to Sunday school (after all, the Ranger's God was a single, powerful concept, not a bunch of silly hymns and recitations), but I settled down in school and my grades improved tremendously.

Perhaps it seems a little simplistic to attribute the gaining of one's moral center to a radio show, but in my case it really did happen that way.

IN 1994, while doing research on the creation of the *Lone Ranger* for my first book, I spent four days with Fran Striker, Jr., the son of the creator. It still surprises me how few people know that an unassuming, imaginative writer from Buffalo, New York created, developed, and wrote the *Lone Ranger, Green Hornet, Sgt. Preston of the Yukon,* and many others. Fran Striker literally wrote thousands of radio shows, novels, and comics featuring these characters, in addition to overseeing the production of records, films, and television treatments.

Fran shared many stories about his father, most if not all, reflecting his loyalty to friends, his compassion toward others, and his integrity as a human being. "To those who listened to his thrice-weekly radio broadcasts," Striker, Jr. reminds us through a biography he wrote of his dad, "[the *Lone Ranger*] was clean living and goodness. He was justice for all. He was the personification of those traits of character that every parent hopes their child will possess, when grown… But to me, all of those admirable traits of character given to the Ranger were so familiar, so recognizable…."

During the last day of our conversation, I noticed a small piece of paper, set in a simple, wooden frame. When I asked Fran about it, he smiled and told me that it was something that had sat on his dad's desk for years. It was the senior Striker's philosophy, a code by which he lived. Fran called it the "I Believes." It was later adapted to become The Lone Ranger Creed:

I believe…

…that to have a friend, a man must be one.

…that all men are created equal and that everyone has within himself the power to help make this a better world.

…that God put the firewood there, but every man must gather and light it for himself.

...in being prepared physically, mentally, and morally to fight when necessary, for that which is right.

...that a man should make the most of what he has.

...that "this government, of the people, by the people, and for the people," shall live always.

...that man should live by the rule of what is best for the greatest number.

...that sooner or later, somewhere, somehow, we must settle with the world and make payment for what we have taken.

...that all things change but truth and that truth alone lives on forever.

...in my creator, my country, and my fellow man.

—FRAN STRIKER

SINCE HER GRADUATION from Barnard College in 1963, Twyla Tharp has choreographed more than one-hundred-twenty-five dances, five Hollywood movies, directed and choreographed two Broadway shows, written two books and received one Tony Award, two Emmy Awards, seventeen honorary doctorates, and numerous grants including the John D. and Catherine T.

MacArthur Fellowship. She is a member of the American Academy of Arts and Sciences and an Honorary Member of the American Academy of Arts and Letters.

> I tend to go on what people *do* rather than what they say. Honesty is a very important commodity. From the very beginning, the necessity was to find material that I could honestly stand behind and say, yes, I understand this. This is necessary for me and it's something that I can belong to and that can belong to me. For any successful artist it's an intense search for what one can honestly believe in. It's not easy to be up front about it, but when you really lock into that, that's what takes conviction to step out with.

Helen Gurley Brown never stops. The author of *Sex and the Single Girl* and editor-in-chief of 47 international editions of *Cosmopolitan* magazine has more energy, interests, and enthusiasm than most 20-somethings. Although she didn't include a story with her reply, her eternal optimism caught my attention. Her response reminds us to focus on the positive rather than the cynicism du-jour.

> Improbable as it sounds, I think the good guys actually win. The bad guys do okay too, in terms of realizing grand schemes, making fortunes, becoming famous (if notoriety is a need). They travel in pasha style commensurate with the fortunes; show up in *People*, all the while grinding down associates, loved ones and enemies, spreading

unhappiness. Inside their heads and hearts, I doubt it's much of a life. Not that all of us don't suffer emotional turmoil at times, but I'd rather be a good guy.

3

value and meaning

Novelist and philosopher Ayn Rand once described ethics as "…a code of values to guide man's choices and actions – the choices and actions that determine the purpose and course of his life."

That's a powerful statement. It says that who we are is determined by what we do. Without some standard of moral judgment we are free to adjust the ethical bar up or down depending on how we perceive the outcome. By using an ethical code, we are providing a benchmark by which to measure ourselves. Codes not only show us what we are doing right but can serve as reminders to do better.

The responses selected center on six common, ethical values which have been distilled from a variety of teachings and philosophies. These are values promoted by my ethics teacher, Michael Josephson and the Josephson Institute of Ethics: Respect, Trustworthiness, Responsibility, Fairness, Citizenship, and Caring.

The ethical principle of Respect means that we not only treat others with courtesy and civility but act with tolerance and acceptance when it comes to individual differences and beliefs. This chapter focuses on perhaps the most basic of all, Respect and its characteristics of courtesy, civility, dignity and acceptance.

Film critic and historian Leonard Maltin describes his principles as "old-fashioned," but sometimes nothing is more sophisticated than reconnecting with those basic tenets of courtesy and respect that we all know and have grown up with.

> I try to live a decent life and do the right thing. I don't see this as being remarkable or particularly praiseworthy; I'm only doing what I was taught to do by my parents. But apparently I am somewhat old-fashioned in my thinking.
>
> When I answer a phone message and the recipient says, with some surprise, "Thanks for returning my call," I realize that he or she doesn't take the gesture for granted. When someone thanks me for sending a snapshot I promised to give them, or acknowledges a thank-you note, I begin to understand that my actions are not commonplace any more.
>
> I believe in things like loyalty and respect, which don't have much place in today's business world. I don't believe that a person has to maintain a cutthroat attitude in order to succeed, even in an office where such tactics normally prevail; one can make a stand without making a fuss. If you have confidence in yourself, and proven abilities, if you know when to speak and when to lay back, you can carve a niche for yourself, maintain your integrity,

and perhaps even set a good example for others around you.

THERE'S A SCENE EARLY IN THE FILM *BULL DURHAM* where the Kevin Costner character is being sized up by the Susan Sarandon character. She's making a choice between two minor league ball players as to whom she'll guide and girlfriend throughout the season. Up to this point, Sarandon – by virtue of her magnetic charm, not to mention an incredible body – has controlled things. Costner's character knows where this is going. He's spent most of his life in baseball, knows his skill-set and can throw-out a steal to second as well as Carlton Fisk. In short, he doesn't need a try-out. That's when he gives his "I believe" speech as he heads for the door. It's a short but memorable rant *against* Astro-turf, the designated hitter, and conspiracy theories, and praise *for* the hangin' curve ball, opening your presents on Christmas Day rather than Christmas Eve, and "...long, slow, deep, *soft*, wet kisses that last three days."

There's an uncomplicated, romantic appeal to certain sports figures. They're frank, sincere, and steadfast, and they don't need an attorney or press secretary to parse their language. (Check out Sparky Anderson's response on page 71.) It's no wonder that many of them not only see life on the field that way but *off* the field as well.

John McCarthy teaches kids the skills they need both on and off the field – focus, persistence, generosity, and humor. He's more interested in teamwork than batting averages, and more concerned with effort than talent. Ultimately, he wants them to understand that bad calls and good calls have a way of evening out both in the game and in life.

McCarthy describes himself as "an average college kid and washout baseball pitcher" in the Baltimore Orioles organization who, in 1992, started his Home Run Baseball Camp for kids. From running what has become the biggest summer camp in Washington D.C. to the critically acclaimed inner city reading and baseball program Elementary Baseball, McCarthy has worked with over 15,000 kids from every socio-economic background. He also serves on the adjunct faculty at Wilson High School, teaching Alternatives to Violence to over one hundred juniors and seniors each year.

McCarthy submitted his own list of "I Believes."

I stand for...success over winning...asking, "How can I help you?"...focusing on one's effort rather than talent...writing thank you notes...having lunch with Headstart students then reading them *Hop on Pop*...firing 3-2 knuckleballs with the bases loaded on the road...riding the waves at Huntington Beach...being a practical idealist...that something is not an ideal until it costs you something...picking up the check...letting neighborhood kids use your lawn for sports...Writing letters to your grandmother...keeping every personal letter someone writes you through the years...bringing flowers for the big shots' secretaries (they're the ones running the show)...shining your shoes...showing up with a fungo for early work...staying late to play stickball with your crew...giving someone a raise before they have to ask for one...giving teenagers their first job...giving a kid in the Dominican Republic his first baseball glove...calling it a tie if you forget the score in ping-pong…backing up a kid when an adult puts his hands on them in anger…backing up your friends…giving memorable toasts at weddings…taking flowers to your kindergarten teacher…learning janitors' names…buying turf shoes for your whole staff…letting a faster group of golfers play through…asking yourself if you are sharing enough every day…repeating kindergarten because you liked it so much…writing a letter to your favorite college professor…working on a service project with a spiritual leader…eye contact…arriving early to work to sweep up and pick up the trash…playing with the pit bull puppies at the pound even though in DC they get put to sleep within 24 hours of arrival…a good poker face…staying up late to watch the west coast ballgames…spending time working with the grounds crew…encouraging kids to eat more fruits and vegetables…being optimistic…going for it on par fives…going entire seasons without saying something negative to an umpire…doing small things in great ways…volunteer teaching at a public school…delivering more than expected.

BILL DANCE has been dispensing fishing advice on television for over thirty years. His humorous, offbeat approach as the host of TNN's *Bill Dance Outdoors* has earned him an avalanche of fans. A partial list of accomplishments includes member of the International Fishing Hall of Fame, 23 national bass titles, 3-time B.A.S.S. Angler of the Year, and spokesperson for at least 25 companies and organizations. Dance's story demonstrates the daily act of treating others with courtesy and kindness.

I believe that one of the most important principles in my life has been one learned from my grandfather at an early age – simply to always treat everyone equally regardless of who they are or their status in life.

Someone once said that the final test of a gentleman is his respect and kindness for those who can be of no possible value to him. A simple smile goes a million miles further than a frown, although there are times for everyone when it's hard to maintain this discipline. At many of the appearances I make, I am required to sign thousands of autographs on caps, t-shirts, tackle boxes, you name it. Listening to "ump-teen" fish stories. "Bill, did I tell you about the big fish I caught last week?" Sometimes I want to reply, "No, and I appreciate that." But, of course, I don't. Even though I've missed a flight or two because of it, I know it's important to that person. After all, people like this are the real reason for my success.

I am always reminded of what my wife Dianne told me long ago, "There is a destiny that calls us brothers. No one goes his way alone. All that we send into the lives of others comes back into our own." When I was just starting my fishing career, I still had a day job that paid the bills – working for a local hardware jobber as a salesman. At one of the big accounts that I had to call on repeatedly, I would always go in the warehouse in the back and there I'd have a Coke with one of the warehouse workers. We'd chat about family, fishing, politics, or whatever, and it became a regular ritual every time I'd go there.

WHAT DO YOU STAND FOR?

Within a year or so, this particular account expanded greatly because they opened three more big stores. All of the purchasing took place at this original store, and much to my surprise someone I know got promoted to senior buying agent. It was my Coke-drinking partner. I imagine I don't have to tell you what salesman started getting the bulk of their business! This certainly wasn't planned on my part and the moral was immediately evident to me. Just being myself and treating the warehouse guy the same as I would treat anyone else paid big dividends although it certainly wasn't my reason for doing so.

I have also always tried to do what I will tell people I will do, regardless of the cost. Sometimes following through can be quite difficult, but it simply must be done…We're only as good as our word. Helping others, especially those less fortunate than me, has always been an important principle to me, and I try to do it whenever possible. There is no greater feeling than doing a little something nice for someone who may never even know it was you who lent a hand.

JENNIFER WESTBROOK is a graduate from Hampton University's Honors College who loves the music of Miles Davis and the writings of Frederick Douglass. Currently a student at Columbia Law School, Westbrook's response reminds us of the importance of recognizing the dignity of others.

A homeless man sat alone on a park bench amongst the horde of people in the park. No one sat on the bench with him because he was distinctly different from the professionals and the tourists. People were reluctant to be near him because his clothes were old, dirty, and torn, and his hair was unkempt. I was amazed that people acted as though he was not there as they carefully walked around him, avoiding his thoughtful stare. As I observed more closely, I realized that they could not possibly help but see and hear him because he was speaking with the power of a great preacher or lecturer. His voice was so strong that it seemed to shake the very bench that I sat on and reverberate throughout the park. Some dismissed his speeches as pure gibberish, but I had an inclination that there was more to this man than met the eye.

One day I sat close by to listen intently to what he was saying, and I was immediately entranced and intrigued. The man rose from his bench and paced the sidewalk. As he approached my bench and began speaking, I saw that he avoided making eye contact with his observers. I sensed that he did this to put his audience at ease by speaking generally to the crowd, even though he directed his lectures to individuals he observed. He seemed to know just what message to deliver. On this particular day, his message was for me. The old man asked, "What is your purpose in life? What makes you different from everyone else in this world? How will you live your life differently from everyone else's?" He walked away, but not before uttering that everyone should believe in something.

I walked the block from my office at the FDIC to that park regularly, and I always saw this man on that same bench. Each time I went there, I noticed him regularly checking his watch. One day I approached him and asked for the time, although I knew what time it was. He paused for a moment, looking shocked that he had been spoken to, and then thoughtfully replied, "It's a quarter to one. God bless you." In that moment I knew he understood that I acknowledged and appreciated him and saw value and meaning in what he committed himself to doing each day.

Ever since that day, I have pondered and reflected upon his words, and I have since realized the importance of believing in something worthwhile. I believe in taking notice of all that is around me, just as I noticed the homeless lecturer that no one truly cared to see. I believe in looking deep inside myself and the world to find greater truth and meaning. I stand for doing the unexpected. I stand for seeing the value in people rather than focusing on adverse opinions and stereotypes. That homeless man was not asking anyone for money or food; rather, he was just asking for someone to acknowledge him. He was looking for a kind heart to show him some dignity and respect.

My principles were tested on that day in the park, and I decided to do the uncommon thing by extending some kindness to that eloquent, yet lonely speaker. From that day on, I did not pass him with trepidation. Instead, I acknowledged him and honored him as a human being. Each day I strive to live by these principles, and I can see and feel the difference it makes in my life and the lives of others.

LAURA-ANN JACKSON'S DREAM is "to work alongside Roger

Ebert." A senior at West Philadelphia Catholic High School, she has moved from creating tales of two-headed dragons to topics ranging from political unrest and social isolation. Her essay for the John Templeton Foundation's Laws of Life essay contest is a remarkable example of discovering and expressing self-respect.

As I wrote my name in the appropriate area, I couldn't help but sneak furtive glances at the "How would you identify yourself?" portion of my college application. I was hoping to find "Please check all that apply" in italics somewhere on the page, but unfortunately my choices were limited to one, which did not include multi-ethnic as an option. Noticing this, I thought about people in similar situations who have been asked, "What are you?" and forced to pick a standard response, which is either based on other people's assumptions or the limiting choices they are given.

When I was in second grade, I knew there were differences among my classmates and me only to the extent that some of us were tall, some short, some plump, some thin. I knew that I was lighter than all of them, but that never seemed to be problematic until the day that I knocked Jeffery Carter out of contention during a "friendly" game of dodge ball. I knew he was angry at having been snagged, but I never expected to hear, "You cheated, white girl!" I gasped and searched for a response while the entire class laughed in unison. I had never been so hurt and humiliated, but the worst was yet to come.

My classmates had grown quite fond of calling me "white girl" as the year progressed, and I got used to being

What Do You Stand For?

alone. I never told my parents or even the teacher for fear that the name-calling would prevail. Unfortunately, my "leave the adults out" theory was incorrect and things continued to get worse. I found derogatory notes in my backpack and even had to pick wads of glue out of my hair on a fairly regular basis. I decided to take matters in my own hands and confront my classmates during one of their rants. I told them that my name was Laura, not "white girl" and proceeded to ask them why they didn't like me. When they said it was because I was white, I countered with "No, I'm not!" As I waited for a response I heard a voice almost whisper, "Then what are you?"

Of course this wouldn't be the last time I was asked that question, but I'm almost thankful to the voice that asked it. It prompted me to ask myself, "What are you?" and when I realized that I didn't have an answer, I had a talk with my parents. My mother's rhetoric told me that I was of Cherokee Indian, Italian, Portuguese, and African-American descent; nonetheless, my seven-year-old mind found it very confusing. Fortunately, my father managed to put it into words I could understand: I was "a little bit of everything."

When I look back at that time in my life, I am filled with mixed emotions. Had it not been for Jeffery Carter constantly pestering me by calling me "white girl," I probably would have had an average second grade experience. On the other hand, I am thankful that this comment led me to begin my journey of self-discovery and awareness though there's still that part of me that wishes it could have been easier. I take that back. If it had been, I don't think I'd be as determined to change people's minds as I am today. The next time someone asks, "What are you?" I think I'll say that I am stronger.

PHOTOGRAPHER MICHAEL COLLOPY looks for the wisdom in the people he photographs. He has gained both insight and recognition for his tritone portraits of world leaders from Pope John Paul II to Margaret Thatcher, entertainers from Luciano Pavarotti to Willie Nelson. His most recent book, *Architects of Peace,* is a study in the quiet dignity and courage of peacemakers from Nelson Mandela to Oakland schoolteacher Ida Jackson. His reply reflects time spent with Mother Teresa and her meaning of acceptance.

I have always attempted to live my life by the principles of love, acceptance, equality, and of a deepening faith. For me, Love is the greatest of these. I have learned and I am learning from young and old, from great spiritual leaders to self-sacrificing unknown individuals that can walk in and out of your life at any moment.

I strive to accept whatever comes into my life and to receive each person and each thing as a gift – even if that gift happens to come to me in the form of suffering. Mother Teresa said, "Take whatever God gives you with a big smile." Mother saw suffering as a gift. For her it was a way to completely align herself with the passion of Christ and in so doing, share in his redemption.

In the course of my friendship with Mother Teresa, I

recognized the fact that she never judged anyone she came into contact with. It always amazed me how individuals would come to Mother and pour out their deepest, sometimes darkest secrets to her. However, Mother always had the same response. She would listen intently. The person in front of her was always the most important to her at that time. She had an incredible ability to see the face of God in each person. Always full of Love. One day I was driving in the car with her on our way to Baltimore with the Sisters and I questioned her about this and said, "Mother with all the different people who come to you, you never seem to judge anyone?" She quickly responded, "I never judge anyone because it would not allow me the time to love them."

4

a simple principle

PEOPLE WHO DEMONSTRATE A CONSISTENCY between ethical principle and ethical practice are worthy of trust. Being trust*worthy* requires more than being honest. It requires us to make reasonable efforts to keep promises and obligations, to demonstrate concern for others through loyalty, and carry out the necessary integrity to resist temptations and pressures and do the right thing even when the personal consequences may cost us.

On more than one occasion, I have learned the importance of being trustworthy in all my relationships.

Several years ago I was playing a board game called *Scruples* with some friends. The object of the game is to draw a card and read a dilemma out loud to the group. You then have to decide which way you will handle that dilemma. How you answer, justifying your decision to the others, determines how many points you receive. If the others believe you answered sincerely, you receive a point. If they *disagree*, they're saying that your response is not consistent with your reputation – as they see it – and you lose a point. The points you receive have nothing to do with an honest *action*.

It's the perceived honesty of your answer that counts.

My turn comes, I draw a card and am surprised to discover that the dilemma described actually happened to me. It outlines a scenario where one choice called for lying to a friend or relative.

Embarrassed, I explained to the others that this actually happened to me and that, unfortunately, I had lied. They didn't buy it. Despite protestations to the contrary, my friends believed me to be nothing less than honest and forthright.

But the consequences of trust can become more than a little uncomfortable even when you're acting in the best interests of others.

In the mid '70s I was working in the post-production end of the film business. Among my many duties was expediting prints at the lab. Over the course of two years I had cultivated a reputation of trust among the people at the lab and was permitted to wander in and out of all kinds of rooms where negatives and prints were stored.

The '70s was a time when home video equipment was just being introduced. Although the technology was available, the equipment was big, bulky and expensive. During this same time, a black market for feature film prints existed. Not the big 35mm prints used in theaters, but the easier, home-friendly 16mm prints. Making and selling those illegal prints was a crime; transporting them across state lines made it a federal offense.

One of my bosses at that time was also president of one of the biggest labs in town. Evidence pointed to a lot of illegal prints coming out of his lab. Because of my affability and access at all times of the day or night, he asked if I would check out the situation, track down who was involved and how it was done. The notion of playing detective appealed to me. However, I wasn't

WHAT DO YOU STAND FOR?

prepared for the consequences of that decision.

To my great surprise, it took very little "detecting" on my part to uncover the information. In fact, the person who was in charge of "bootlegging" the prints approached *me*! "If you ever have any interested clients," he said, "let me know." Claiming to have never seen a 35-to-16mm reduction print made, I asked him to show me the process. Late one night, he showed me into the print room and the area where the negatives for films in current release were stored. It took me all of maybe one week to put everything together

But something gnawed at me.

After giving an update on my progress, I asked my boss if others were involved in helping to catch the thieves. He assured me that my information was but one piece of corroborating information.

Around that time I had been invited to a company picnic that the "bootlegger" and his family also attended. The man had become a friend and seemed sincerely devoted to his wife and kids. This was in a time, as well as a business, where I observed more than a little cheating going on.

The following Monday I was contacted by a detective on the case who came into my office and shut the door. "We're ready to close in on these guys," he said, "and this is what I want you to do. Tell him that you have a client who will be calling to order some prints."

A day later, the "bootlegger" called back to tell me that my "client" had ordered quite a number of prints, that it seemed unusual, and that it would take a few days to complete the order. I was beginning to feel uneasy about the whole thing due to the volume of the order and the speed with which the whole process was taking place. "Relax," the detective told me. "We do this all the time."

A few days later, he instructed me to stay away from the lab the next day. Ironically, the "bootlegger" called while the detective was still in my office. He, too, was concerned by the large order, but said "if *you* say he's okay, Jim. He's okay." All I could think of from that moment on was this man's wife and kids from the picnic and it bothered me.

Clearly, the people responsible were criminals. And just as clearly, I was doing the right thing by turning them in, but these guys were not your typical Clint Eastwood, *Dirty Harry* crooks who you root to see shot by the end of the film. These guys had become my friends, friends who had families.

Now I know what you're thinking – "Wake up and smell the developer, Jim! These guys were crooks who were stealing the livelihood of others." All true. Wouldn't argue with you. They deserve what they get. But the image of the "bootlegger's" family banged in my brain as I spent the next day hanging around the office, avoiding the lab.

The following afternoon, one of my guys returned to the office with a load of prints under his arm. "Man, you should have been there," he said. "There were FBI guys all over the place! And you should have seen it when [the "bootlegger"] was led away in cuffs. It was like an episode from some crime show!"

Despite the fact that I gave one of the great reacting jobs in my life, whenever anyone approached me about the incident – and everyone was talking about it for weeks – the whole thing made me sick to my stomach. Worse yet was the realization that I could never tell anyone for fear that I would be looked on as someone who would turn *anyone* in if I noticed the slightest indiscretion. So, I kept my mouth shut. Have never told anyone, until now.

Standing up for what we know to be right can be difficult, but if one can summon the moral courage necessary, the results can provide moral clarity for the next ethical decision.

SAM BROADNAX has had a varied career. After serving as a fighter pilot for the Tuskegee Airmen in World War II, he was a lab technician and an engineering technician and retired as a newscaster at KSFO radio in San Francisco. Broadnax currently serves as president of the San Francisco Bay Chapter of Tuskegee Airmen, Inc. Among the programs the chapter sponsors is an annual Summer Flight Academy for "at risk" kids 14-18 years of age. His response focuses on the outcome of acting in an honest and forthright way.

I have for years been guided by the principle of Trust. The given word, the handshake, the written signature, or a combination of all three form the leading principle which has been molded into my conduct. It is this unvarying trust that gives substance to character and an unequivocal meaning to respect. I speak not of trust that means…"I trust you are well," or "We trust you will do the right thing."

When I was a teenager, my foster mother once accused me of physically harming our miniature French poodle. Despite my protestations of innocence, my punishment was the silent treatment for more than a week. Then it so happened that a neighbor down the street inquired how Fritz was since she had seen him in a furious dogfight with an animal four times his size. When my foster mother returned, she found the hole in the fence that Fritz had used in his untimely escape. The truth unfolded in obvious order and I was forgiven. I was told that I would always be trusted from that moment on. The effect of that incident has remained to this day an important segment in my foundation of principles.

As a child actor, Dick Jones played more kid roles in all types of dramatic and western pictures than probably anyone in the movie industry. In 1938, Walt Disney chose the 11-year-old Jones to be the voice of *Pinocchio* in the animated film classic. His motion picture, radio, and television career spans 55 years; he appeared in nearly 100 movies and over 200 television productions. Among the most memorable are the *Our Gang Comedies, Stella Dallas, Destry Rides Again, Young Mister Lincoln,* and my own favorite, the bright-eyed but savvy Senate page in *Mr. Smith Goes to Washington.*

I think my principles and things I stand for are, more or less, based on my interest and love in the Boy Scouts of America. I still believe in the oath – "On my honor I will do my best to do my duty to God and my country…to help other people at all times; to keep myself physically strong, mentally awake, and morally straight."

The Scout law goes on further than that – "A Scout is loyal, trustworthy…" Trustworthy. That goes all the way back to another of my major principles of honesty. I believe in rigorous honesty.

When Jock O'Mahoney and I started *The Range Rider* [television series], that very first day that we got together we made a pact that we were going to do all of our own stunts. Jock O' said to me, "We're going out on the road and we're going to see an awful lot of little kids. And they're all going to look at you starry-eyed, 'Did you do this? Did you do that? Did you jump off that cliff? Did you tackle that guy off the horse?' And we can look 'em right in the eye and say, "Yes, we did!"

We had to put some action in because we weren't singin' cowboys, and we didn't have any trick horses or anything like that. We were the first ones to do a "Bulldog" horse fall in one shot. We were the first ones to do a "Double Bulldog" on four other guys. We would immediately lose our hats so that they could see that it was us and not a double. Did you ever see Gene Autry doing that? We were the only ones who could, and we're the only ones who did! When you could look at [those kids] and honestly say, "Yes we did that," without giving them any malarkey, that felt good inside.

JAMES NIXON, an earlier contributor, offered this story of honesty about golfer Bobby Jones.

While competing in a tournament back in the '20s, Jones hit his ball into the woods. After hitting it back out, he announced to his fellow competitors that he had incurred a one-stroke penalty because the ball had moved while he was addressing it. No one had witnessed the violation. Jones could easily have ignored it, and no one ever would have known. Yet he didn't and went on to lose the tournament by one shot. It is this spirit of personal honesty which makes golf such a great game and which tests the very essence of anyone's moral fiber. Let me play just one round of competitive golf with a person, and I can tell you volumes about his or her character. Invariably, if a person cheats at golf, he cheats in life. It may not be in huge ways, but it will be dishonest nonetheless. Golf may only be a game, but as a test of one's ethical underpinning, there is no equal.

ONE, AMONG MANY STORIES I RECEIVED about simple honesty, came from Michael Braunstein, the Director of North American Operations with BPP Professional Training, a company that provides study support for those in pursuit of actuarial exams.

I have come across many sets of principles during the course of my life – the Golden Rule, the Scout Law, the Six Pillars of Character, Ten Commandments. Though all of them work well as principles to live by, my own approach has been simpler. I simply try to do what I believe is the right thing to do. I am convinced that, deep down, we all know what that is, and I believe that, if we all followed that simple principle, the world would be a better place. I wish

WHAT DO YOU STAND FOR?

I could say that I have always been true to that principle; I cannot. However, I can share a recent story in which I do feel quite good about my actions.

Back in 1988, I proposed to my wife and gave her a rather expensive diamond engagement ring. We were subsequently married and now have three children. One night, in late 1996 while my wife was changing the baby, she discovered to her horror, that the stone from her ring had come out of the setting. When I arrived home, she was so upset that she couldn't even get the words out to tell me what happened. Her emotions were so strong that I thought something terrible had happened to one of the kids. I was relieved when I finally learned that the issue involved the ring and not one of the children. With every light in the house turned off and with flashlight in hand, I covered every square inch of the floor, countertop, furniture, etc., all to no avail.

Fortunately, the ring was insured and, though there was much sentimental value lost, we were able to replace the diamond with a very similar stone. The jeweler did a terrific job of putting the ring back together, and I did my best to give this new ring some sentimentality of its own by "re-proposing" to my wife in another romantic setting. Though it wasn't quite the same, it somehow seemed okay.

About a year later, after putting the kids to bed one night, I headed up to my third floor office to do some work. As I got to the top of the stairs, there on the floor was the diamond, just sitting there and appearing at first to be just a small piece of glass.

We now theorize that the stone fell out of the setting while my wife was moving some seasonal clothes from one closet to the other. I was amazed when I first saw it and, initially, was not sure what to do. I wasn't even sure that I wanted to tell my wife. Here was something valued at nearly $10,000 and nobody but me knew about it.

Moments later, I realized that my wife would be thrilled and that I had to let her know. The next question was, what do we do now? Do we tell the insurance company? Do we return this stone? Do we hide it in the safe deposit box? Do we sell it? In telling the story to friends, I always joke about it. "The choice," I say, "is to do the right thing or burn in hell for eternity."

The decision turned out to be an easy one. We called the insurance company the next day and told them the good news. Though I expected them to be surprised at my honesty, they told me that they get many such calls, long after claims are settled. I've learned that I'm not any better than anyone else. The world does behave appropriately in many cases.

The insurance company offered us two options. We could return either stone or purchase the found stone at what they termed "salvage value" which is all they would get anyway. The deal was too good to pass up, and our finances were sufficient that we could take advantage of the latter deal. For less than a third of its retail value, we kept the stone. I had it set in a pendant, and, on the 10th anniversary of our engagement, I secretly arranged for my wife and me to be at the very location where we were first engaged and was able to surprise her with it.

We now have two diamond engagement pieces, and, some day, each of our two daughters will get one. We feel good about what we did, and what was once a very sad moment has become a most delightful story.

CHERRIE GRECO began her professional career as a public educator in 1969 and has teaching credentials from eight U.S. states. In 1991 she moved into educational programs in prison such as gang education, and Adult Basic Education and produced a series of educational video programs for segregated offenders. Currently serving as the Director, Division of Training, for the Colorado Department of Corrections, she was asked to represent the Department of Corrections as its liaison and lobbyist to Colorado's Legislative General Assembly. Cherrie's story reminds us that most of us have some experience from our past that we can't think about without flinching, but those events can help shape our future actions.

I remember the day when one of my classmates brought to school a bird's nest containing a tiny robin's egg. I was eight. As members of the class, we were cautioned by our teacher not to touch the little egg; that being so fragile, the egg would surely break in our hands.

The first bell rang signaling everyone to take their seats. As the children hustled noisily about, I could not resist the temptation. I had to touch the tiny little egg. Gingerly I picked it up from the nest; and, just as my teacher had predicted, the egg broke in my hands. I was horrified as I watched the yellow liquid drip through my fingers. Amazingly, no one noticed.

I left the room (without permission – a violation of an important class rule) and hurried into the restroom. Quickly, I put my hands under the faucet and desperately washed away the evidence. An older girl, (in the eighth grade) came in. For some reason I felt compelled to tell her that my classmates and I had been working on crafts, and I needed to wash my hands. She looked at me, dumb-founded; I now know that guilt motivated my urgency to babble something, anything.

When I returned to the classroom, the teacher repri-manded me for being tardy. All morning I secretly fretted that my crime would be found out. Just before first recess the teacher looked into the nest, and with shock and hor-ror in her voice, announced that the little bird egg was bro-ken. The boys and girls cried out in unison, "Ooohh…"

The teacher asked us what we knew. She quizzed for clues, which would point to the guilty party. No one offered any hints about who the guilty person could be. She asked us to lay our heads on our desks. She promised that if the person responsible would just raise his or her hand, that she would not identify that child to the rest of the class. I didn't raise my hand. My arms easily weighed one hundred pounds each. The teacher dismissed us for recess, and the child who brought the nest to school was the recipient of unexpected sympathy.

Until this writing, I never shared the memory with anyone. Fear and later shame were too intense for me to even articulate the story.

In the big scheme of things, this incident is a typical childhood indiscretion; something so minor that, even failing to own up to the deed, would not contribute to choosing a poor path in life. What the example *did* do for me, however, was help plot the road map, which has guided my choices.

JOHN ZOGBY is CEO of Zogby International, a Polling Market Opinion Research Company. His company has polled, researched, and consulted for a wide range of business, media, government, and political groups including Microsoft, CISCO Systems, Philip Morris, NBC News, Gannett News Service, St. Jude's Children's Research Hospital, MCI, and Reuters America, as well as the United States Census Bureau. Zogby's response raises a common question: do you tell 100% of the truth 100% of the time?

> I was only 12 years old when my father died. He was an immigrant from Lebanon and ran a grocery store. The one abiding principle he taught me was to always be truthful with family, colleagues, and customers. It sounds so simple and yet we are all constantly challenged to allow other needs to trump the need for truth. I have found that when I tell it straight, I don't have to worry about keeping my story straight, whether I have been consistent or whether I have created a web that actually causes more problems for myself and others.
>
> However, there are many occasions when you're conducting this business, or any other kind of business – there

is a sausage-making process, something that takes place in the back room – that the customer doesn't necessarily need to know about.

I remember one time when I was nine; my dad worked seven days a week in a supermarket. He went to the grocery store on Sunday just to do some bookkeeping, took me with him, and a woman stopped in and said, "Can I pick up a few items, Joe?" "By all means," he said. She picked up a few things and said, "Do you have fresh donuts, by any chance?" And he said, "Oh, do I have fresh donuts!" He went to the back of the store, handed me a dollar and said, "Go out the back door, go across the street and buy some donuts and come back through the back door."

Now, my father may not have been 100% truthful, and this is the guy who taught me to be truthful above all else! The bottom line was, the lady wanted fresh donuts, and because she didn't really care where the donuts came from, he was delivering great customer service.

What am I getting at? There are times when you're dealing with a client and that client may want to micromanage every aspect of doing the poll. And, we say to them, you don't want to do that because then you will know the "truth," and sometimes the truth is a lot of people hang up on us or tell us to go jump in the lake. Sometimes there's a little glitch here or there in the statistical analysis and we have to have it re-done. So, sometimes there are some things that challenge truth, in its absolute.

What we say is that we are working on other projects and have been delayed – which happens to be true because we always have other work going on. The thing is, at what point does telling the 100% truth become counterproductive when you can be better served by just simply holding back as opposed to telling a flat-out lie. A flat-out lie would be, "Hey, everything is going well. We'll get it to you at three o'clock like we said."

Sometimes clients can cause a conflict with our responsibility to the truth. One time, we had a group that wanted us to do a poll on the Confederate Flag. And they were pro-Confederate Flag in Mississippi. I took the approach that it's a legitimate issue, and I asked the question honestly and fairly, "How do people feel about that in Mississippi?" Well, there were two problems. One was when the group told us that they were certainly hoping that the result would be favorable to them. Bells started going off. Number two, we checked their website and saw some paraphernalia for sale that was not terribly consistent with how we saw ourselves as, not only a polling firm, but as human beings and Americans. Then we told them to take a walk.

I have done work for the ultra-Right, the ultra-Left and all points in between. We've rejected some on both sides when we thought it just simply wasn't consistent with our image – to be fair, honest brokers of information.

DENNY **B**RAUER is one of the most respected and successful professional bass fishermen in the country. A thirteen-time winner on the highly competitive B.A.S.S. tournament trail, he holds the single season money winnings record on the B.A.S.S. circuit and is also first in career winnings with over a million dollars.

I have tried to treat other people the way I wanted to be treated and above all be as honest as possible. I think those two things take care of everything else.

A recent example happened in 1998, during the Bassmasters Classic, [where] I won the World Championship of Bass Fishing. The Classic is the most prestigious tournament in our industry. The lure used to win can become an instant success because of the exposure from the tournament.

It would have been real easy to make a story up in regards to what lure I caught the fish on for immediate financial gain. My whole career I have always stated exactly what I caught my fish on. I was not about to change my policy. I told the truth, and I think the press and fans really appreciated the honest statement about my success. Fortunately, my lure sponsor had me design an improved version of the lure I won on. This ended up being a great deal because now anglers have a better fish-catching lure. So it worked out for everyone in the long run.

ALAN GREENSPAN has a unique way of speaking. In fact, the Chairman of the Federal Reserve's statements before Congress are *so* unique that it frequently takes the better part of several cable news programs and an army of analysts to examine and explain them to the rest of us! Even then there are often disagreements among the "experts." However, in a commencement address made to Harvard graduates in June of 1999, Greenspan quite plainly points out what *is* important and why.

"I presume that I could offer all kinds of advice to today's graduates from my half-century in private business and government. I could urge you all to work hard, save, and prosper. And I do. But transcending all else is being principled in how you go about doing those things.

"It is decidedly not true that 'nice guys finish last,' as that highly original American baseball philosopher, Leo Durocher, was once alleged to have said.

"I do not deny that many appear to have succeeded in a material way by cutting corners and manipulating associates, both in their professional and in their personal lives. But material success is possible in this world and far more satisfying when it comes without exploiting others. The true measure of a career is to be able to be content, even proud, that you succeeded through your own endeavors without leaving a trail of casualties in your wake.

"I cannot speak for others whose psyches I may not be able to comprehend, but, in my working life, I have found no greater satisfaction than achieving success through honest dealings and strict adherence to the view that for you to gain, those you deal with should gain as well. Human relations – be they personal or professional – should not be zero sum games.

"And beyond the personal sense of satisfaction, having a reputation for fair dealing is a profoundly practical virtue. We call it 'good will' in business and add it to our balance sheets.

"Trust is at the root of any economic system based on mutually beneficial exchange. In virtually all transactions, we rely on the word of those with whom we do business. Were this not the case, exchange of goods and services could not take place on any reasonable scale. ...Without mutual trust, and market participants abiding by a rule of law, no economy can prosper."

STEVE AMBRA is Assistant Director, New Hampshire Technical Institute Library in Concord. He's also an adjunct professor who teaches Contemporary Ethical Issues, Introduction to Film History, and Advanced Film Studies. In 1975, Ambra found himself "...caught on the horns of an ethical dilemma involving loyalty."

I was a doctoral student in philosophy at a university in which the department was torn between those people who supported the old department head and those who had successfully ousted him as chair and were now seeking his involuntary retirement from the department.

Going against the administration meant the loss of the appearance of safety with the administration in power (siding with the "winning" team) which oversaw each student's credentials primarily through the enforcement of departmental requirements (i.e. requirements to take certain courses versus waiver of those courses, "suggested" additional courses necessary toward completion of the degree, etc.)

The personal relationship I developed with the now

former department head helped me to decide to attend the institution. To abandon him, and the decision to attend which I equated with my interaction with him, was to me intellectually dishonest, mercenary and just plain wrong.

I asked myself a very simple question: which answer would allow me to live with myself? Even though the position was difficult, the decision was not: loyalty and intellectual honesty motivated my decision not to abandon the former chair. By making the choice I did I could live with my decision and myself. The value of loyalty was underscored as a guiding principle in my life. It caused me to embark on a different career path, which has culminated in my librarianship, my teaching ethics and film and coaching soccer.

ON SCREEN DOUGLAS FAIRBANKS, JR. seemed inspired playing suave, sophisticated, larger-than-life characters – the swashbuckling Irishman in *The Fighting O'Flynn*, the swashbuckling villain in *The Prisoner of Zenda*, and swashbuckling twins, no less, in *The Corsican Brothers*. Off screen, Fairbanks led a much more complex life than any of his characters. Six weeks before Pearl Harbor, the star of *Gunga Din* began his naval service and rose to commander during his six-year service. For Fairbanks, patriotism and duty to one's country are the ultimate expressions of loyalty.

What do I stand for? To follow and obey the Ten Commandments as closely as my circumstances and individual character have allowed, admitting that full unwavering obedience is a goal which few are able to achieve.

A 'moment of principle': Voluntarily putting my personal life and career on the line for six years by participating in close combat in WW II.

To say that Fairbanks' actions were above and beyond the call of duty is an understatement. Unlike some Hollywood "heroes" who never heard a shot fired, Fairbanks spent most of his time in harm's way. He saw combat in Europe and the Mediterranean. His assignments included serving under British Admiral Lord Mountbatten in a commando operation as well as participating in Psychological Operations for the U.S. Navy Beach Jumper units.

One event, toward the end of the war with Japan, stands out. It comes from Fairbanks' autobiography, *A Hell of a War*:

"Jim Forrestal, our first secretary of defense, had examined various plans to end the war with Japan and dismissed mine in a brief memo declaring: 'On the whole it may be said that the extreme, difficult and hazardous means proposed by Commander Fairbanks are entirely unnecessary to convince Japanese leaders that they are on the verge of defeat.'

"[Eugene S.] Dooman [assistant secretary of state for Japanese affairs, and the chairman of the committee for formulating surrender policies] encouraged me to rewrite still another idea in 'officialese.' Consequently, my next top-secret memo...included ideas for a draft text of a proclamation by the United States, United Kingdom, and Chinese heads of state to the people of Japan. The basic idea was that a Japanese agreement to post surrender peace terms would be more generally acceptable if we were to agree to retention of their emperor as head of state.

"To Gene Dooman's quiet surprise and my silent astonishment the plan, this time with no authorship attached, was first approved by Secretary Hull and Ambassador Grew, who then showed it to President Truman... This was the document that might be called the preface or the protocol which President Truman and Secretary of War Stimson took with them to Potsdam and showed to Prime Minister Churchill. It emerged practically unchanged as the preamble to the later Potsdam Declaration of Japan. What was then regarded as the essential paragraph included the words '...*the establishment of a responsible government of a character representative of the Japanese people. This may include a constitutional monarchy under the present dynasty....*'

"More than six years later, during the...Senate's Judiciary Committee in September 1951, dear Gene Dooman was asked the 'how and why' of the whole background of the Potsdam Declaration, outlining the Allied peace terms for the Japanese.

"'MR. DOOMAN (to the Committee Chairman): ...I would like to put on record here that the preamble to the Potsdam Declaration was taken from a document prepared by Douglas Fairbanks, who was then in the Navy Department in the Psychological Warfare Department.

"'THE CHAIRMAN: Douglas Fairbanks?

"'MR. DOOMAN: The movie actor.

"'MR. SOURWINE: Father or son?

"'MR. DOOMAN: Son.

"'MR. SOURWINE: Douglas Fairbanks, Jr.

"'MR. DOOMAN: Yes.

"Someone later reported a barely audible 'Good God!'"

During his years of service, Douglas Fairbanks received the French Croix de Guerre with palm for his part in the amphibious assault on southern France; the Italian War Cross for Military Valor; the British Distinguished Service Cross as well as the U.S. Legion of Merit with bronze *V* (for valor) attachment. Years later, then Vice Admiral H. Kent Hewitt, Commander, Amphibious Force, U.S. Atlantic Fleet said: "It appeared to me that he was constantly trying to contribute the maximum toward winning the war, and making good as a naval officer, while avoiding any appearance of capitalizing in any way on either his own or his father's reputation as an actor. Fairbanks' service throughout was distinguished and a credit to himself and to his country."

AFTER ENJOYING GOOD FOOD AND FRIENDS FOR YEARS, Chuck Williams went to France to experience the food and culture, returning with the idea of opening up a store that would sell the same quality cookware that those same fine restaurants and chefs used. Since the start of his modest store in Sonoma, California, the Williams-Sonoma stores and catalog have become the gold standard for anything to do with the kitchen. Williams' answer demonstrates that one component of a good reputation is keeping your word.

I can think of six words that express what I stand for – service,

WHAT DO YOU STAND FOR?

quality, creativity, integrity, knowledge and simplicity. They are the principles I have lived by and are the principles that the first small Williams-Sonoma was based on over 40 years ago.

In January 1959 on my first attempt at finding and buying kitchenware, I went to Paris, not knowing a thing about buying or importing in a foreign country. After a couple of days of hopeless encounters in shops and offices, I found that I needed a buying agent. With the help of a friend I was sent to see Mr. Andre Friedman of an old established buying office.

He welcomed me and listened to my story of just opening a small shop in San Francisco with the dream of having a French kitchenware shop. He said that they had no experience with kitchenware manufacturers but that he might consider working with me. He then said, "But first, before we go any further I must know, who are you? I don't know you. What is your credit rating? What are your references?" I replied that I knew nothing about credit ratings and references. He finally said, "Oh, go away and come back in a half hour and I will tell you if we can work together."

So, a little dejected, I departed, walked the neighborhood for a half hour and returned. He greeted me with, "Okay, let us get started. You are okay." But, I said, "How do you know? What made up your mind?" "Oh it is very simple," he said, "I simply telephoned the Chase National Bank in New York, and they checked with Dun and Bradstreet and your bank. They reported back that you are okay."

At that moment he became my buying agent on an open

account basis, which is unusual in the import-export business. No letters of credit or guarantee, just a bill sent to me after receiving the merchandise. It was a "moment of mutual trust" that I have never forgotten, and each year thereafter on my return to Paris on a buying trip, he always took me to one of his favorite restaurants for a lunch to renew that feeling of mutual trust. His company remained my buying agent for more than 20 years until his heirs closed the business.

It was an experience that would probably not happen today, which makes me treasure it even more. This really adds another word – *Trust* – to the six that I gave you, which makes seven words that express what I stand for and live by.

I MET DAVE PARKER while researching the origin and background of the Lone Ranger for my first book. Parker's doctoral dissertation, *A Descriptive Analysis of the Lone Ranger as a Form of Popular Art* became my bible for how and why the Lone Ranger and Tonto acted out of a set of ethical principles.

Beginning his career in broadcasting back in 1948 as a radio actor on *The Lone Ranger*, *Green Hornet*, and other shows, he has been a TV producer-director at NBC and writer for numerous award-winning programs. At the time of the events of his story, he was president of a documentary film company at Universal City. Parker's story raises an interesting question: How important is it to keep a promise to someone whom you will probably never see again?

Back in the '60s when much of America was terrified of

"kids-using-drugs," our film production company was hired to create a film that would really turn the kids off about drug use of any kind. But because we all knew that so-called "scare tactics" really didn't work, and any phony "Hollywood" approach would be hooted off the screen, I set out to find a *real* drug-using girl who would let us join her life and see what drugs had done (and were still doing) to her!

Clearly, she had to be appealing, and willing to let us film her drug-using moments as well as her daily routine. For legal reasons, she had to be at least 20 though I hoped she'd look younger. I didn't want a last stage burnout who'd been living in the gutter, but someone the kids would find authentic, someone who'd appear honest and trusting – a person with whom high school kids could identify. But, of course, someone who was still using drugs, preferably some hard-core stuff like heroin, LSD, or something else the kids might regard as "heavy shit," as they said then!

After searching the known hangouts of drug using kids like San Francisco's Haight-Ashbury, I finally found her with some other kids in a run down coffee house. She was everything I'd been hoping for – sad, forlorn, vulnerable, with a waif-like sweetness I knew would really "read" for the audience. She told me her name was "Marcie" and she'd run away from home. The more I interviewed her the more appealing she became. I asked her what kind of drugs she used, and she admitted she was hooked on heroin or "smack" as she called it.

Fact was, Marcie was great for my purpose, and I simply had to have her story in the film. After I felt I'd gained her trust, I told her about the film and asked her if she'd be willing to let us shoot some of her experiences in "the drug world." "Yeah, I guess," she said. "You're a really nice guy – not like those other film jerks you see around here."

Back at the studio I rejoiced that we'd found our STAR! She'd actually let us film her buying a variety of drugs and best of all, using them! And she was so honest and believable! Yes sir folks, this film was going to win a ton of prizes and help our little company get famous.

"One thing I won't do for you, though," she said. "I won't shoot up smack. Grass, other stuff, OK, but no way am I going to shoot up on your camera."

At just that moment I'd agree to anything as long as Marcie would be in the film, so I said, "Hey, no problem!" "That's cool," she said. "I wouldn't do this for anyone else. But I trust you."

So we filmed Marcie all over the place. We filmed her buying LSD and mescaline, and grass by the bushel. We filmed her hitchhiking and sleeping on a park bench. We saw her smoking pot and dropping acid. We saw her panhandling for money, and wandering aimlessly on the beach at Santa Cruz. But the story needed a solid payoff, something really dramatic – a real climactic moment that would leave the kids in the audience shaken. Something that would loft our little company into national attention. Shooting smack would be ideal.

We'd get Marcie in a sleazy motel room with dim

lighting, sitting all alone on a bed with her candle, needle and spoon. She'd tie off a vein and stick the needle in as we zoomed in for a real scary close up of the needle in her arm! Then we'd cut back to a wide shot showing her almost in silhouette as she nodded off as the music rose to a tender tag. Yeah man, tears!

But she'd said she wouldn't do that!

With deadlines approaching, I finally determined the solution. I could fake it. I'd get another girl with a similar build and hairstyle, and shoot her in silhouette. Nobody would ever know the difference. And of course I'd never tell Marcie who'd feel betrayed and hate me forever if she knew. But hey, she was just a run-away street kid. What difference would it make?

So, that's what I did!

The scene was terrific. Everything I'd imagined. The perfect payoff that would tell the horrific drug story like it really was. As I sat in the editing room, visions of awards flickered in my head. Film editors are almost never impressed with the footage they work with, but this time was different. "Just great!" said my guy. "How'd you ever get her to do that?" "Oh," said I with convincing humility, "sometimes you just get lucky, I guess."

Bottom line – I had a great show with the promise of many sales nationwide *if* I left the last scene intact. It was highly unlikely I'd ever see Marcie again; she was just a "street kid." Nobody would ever know. Nobody but me! I'd know and I'd hate the deception that brought me the awards and the money. Besides, Marcie trusted me. I just couldn't betray her.

So the show went to its final printing without the scene I'd shot. The show was much weaker, and it didn't win any awards, and it didn't do very well in sales, and those few who knew what I'd done asked, "Why in God's name did you toss that great scene? It would have made all the difference!"

What do I stand for? Maybe the simple honesty of giving my word. Maybe the wish to see myself as a guy with some sense of honor. Marcie trusted me and I couldn't betray her, even though she'd probably never know. I know THIS – I've never regretted my decision.

SOME PEOPLE THINK that the only way you can teach college athletes and build a winning basketball season is to intimidate, bully and demean. It's a good thing John Wooden and his students never paid much attention to that kind of "conventional" wisdom. Always there to support, encourage, and congratulate, Coach Wooden directed his UCLA Basketball teams to 10 NCAA titles – including 7 in a row – and achieved an amazing lifetime wining percentage of 81.5%. In 1934, Wooden coined his own definition for success – "Peace of mind which is a direct result of self-satisfaction in knowing you did your best to become the best of which you are capable of becoming." Through word and deed, John Wooden taught his student players how to be successful in life.

Although I am imperfect and have failed at times, I have tried to live up to the creed that my father gave to me when

I graduated from a small three-room country grade school in 1924. He gave me a small card with a verse on one side and the seven-point creed on the other and simply said, "Son, try to live up to these."

THE VERSE

Four things a man must learn to do
If he would make his life more true:
To think without confusion – clearly,
To love his fellow man – sincerely,
To act from honest motives – purely,
To trust in God and Heaven – securely.

THE CREED

1. Be true to yourself.
2. Make each day your masterpiece.
3. Help others.
4. Drink deeply from good books.
5. Make friendship a fine art.
6. Build a shelter against a rainy day.
7. Pray for guidance and give thanks for your blessings every day.

In April of 1948, I had decided to accept a position at the University of Minnesota, providing they could work out a problem with their Board of Regents. They were to call me by five o'clock one afternoon, as UCLA, my second choice, was to call me by 6 p.m. for an answer. The Minnesota representatives failed to call, and when the

UCLA people called on time, I accepted their position.

The Minnesota people called an hour later and said that everything was all set. I told them that, since they had not called on time and UCLA had, I accepted the position at UCLA and could not go back on my word. The Minnesota representative informed me that an unexpected and unseasonable snowstorm had delayed their getting to a telephone.

As Abraham Lincoln, my favorite American, said, "Things work out best for those who make the best of the way things work out."

In 1951, a Mount Vernon, New York housewife, four months pregnant, wanted to earn some extra money. Browsing through a variety of women's magazines, she came up with the idea of selling a personalized handbag and belt. Using $2,000 of wedding gift money, she designed a handbag and belt, bought an embossing machine and a $495 ad in *Seventeen* magazine. Today, the Lillian Vernon catalogs generate over a quarter of a billion dollars in annual sales. Keeping a promise to her customers, no matter what it takes, remains central to her philosophy.

> My integrity is the principle I most cherish. If you don't guard and maintain it, no one else will. That's why my company bears my name – because I personally stand behind every product we sell. I offer a 100% money back guarantee, even ten years after a purchase. I want my customers to be satisfied. After more than 50 years, I believe my strong sense of integrity has helped me to build this

loyal following. I also feel that it is important that I set an example for my staff as a positive role model.

1983 marked a dramatic growth in our business, so much so, I found myself having to expand our facilities and add to the payroll. Inventory was building and our old computer system could not keep up with an 80% increase in orders. Fulfillment of orders became slow and updating the system would cost millions. We had expanded so fast that we were playing catch-up; only we couldn't catch up rapidly enough.

I consulted my lawyers, accountants, and labor experts, but good recommendations do not always come fast enough. I found myself in a hole. My entire inventory – some $20 million worth – was piling up in our warehouses. We are a very seasonal business with 70% of our sales and 100% of our profits coming during the second half of the year. My advisors were telling me that I could not meet on-time Christmas delivery for my customers. I actually feared for my company's future.

I had grown up never knowing what the next day would bring. I'd watched Nazi thugs throw my brother down a staircase, evict my family from our house, and cause my father to rebuild two businesses and his life from scratch. I was forced to learn new languages, make new friends, adjust to new cultures. Now, once again, I faced fear and uncertainty. In many ways the business was my life; now I faced losing it. It was a crushing thought.

I was determined not to declare bankruptcy nor would I fall short on my customer promise of "satisfaction guaranteed." I was not used to debt or breaking my promises. Nervously, I walked into my bank president's office and admitted that my company was in trouble, and it needed an immediate infusion of cash. I got a $13 million loan, and we were able to pay our bills quickly as the busiest season started. We contracted for the installation of a more sophisticated computer system that would update the way we ran the business in the future.

That season, however, I was advised that we could not offer timely Christmas delivery to our customers. I was told that trying to do so would be impractical. I was faced with the moral dilemma of, knowingly, breaking my promise. I could not and would not break my word. To this day I'll never forget the Christmas of '83.

Starting in November and going through December, our distribution center became a 24 hour, 7 day a week operation. We hired additional workers and a management staff creating round-the-clock shifts. Employee rank ceased to matter, and every company employee, including vice presidents, rotated overtime shifts at our warehouse, picking and packing customer orders. The last seven days before Christmas, we stopped every company function that required the use of our computer system.

Processing customer orders was the *only* priority. We shipped every customer's order next day air priority, absorbing all the extra costs. We shipped such a large volume that Federal Express designated planes for our exclusive use. While we did not realize 100% customer satisfaction for all our customers, we came much closer than anyone thought

What Do You Stand For?

possible. We spared no expense to keep my promise of...customer satisfaction guaranteed.

Hall of Fame baseball manager Sparky Anderson was one of the first to respond. No one could ever accuse Sparky of being long-winded. Although his principles seem brief in print, they're long on impact over a lifetime.

1. I don't live by the wallet. I live by the truth.
2. Principle to me is when you give your word, always keep it.

5

trust and confidence

Ethics is not about what we say or what we intend, it's about what we *do*.

This is the heart of Integrity – demonstrating a consistency between ethical principle and practice.

Who we are is never more clearly revealed than in the daily moments of our lives. How we respond to some of those moments reveals whether we stand up for our principles or rationalize our way around them. Sometimes, though, even the rationalizing moments can serve as an example to do better.

Sophomore English, and I was facing a last-minute change – the most intimidating teacher on campus. Mr. Freeman was the tough-as-nails track coach and algebra teacher who could smell deceit. Blessed with the quickest hands in the business, if he even *thought* you were in the middle of a lie, you quickly felt a hard sting across your face that you'd never forget.

In algebra class, Freeman delighted in taunting anyone who was slow until you either solved the problem or had to tolerate him standing next to you as he explained every single step. He was this way with all school activities.

During a fundraiser, homeroom teachers would ask their students to sell raffle tickets. In Freeman's class it was a requirement. Two days before Christmas break, he dropped two ticket books on everyone's desk. When I respectfully explained that I would be leaving for California for the Holidays, Freeman just said, "I guess you'll have to sell your tickets in the next two days." When I politely pointed out that selling the tickets was an option not a requirement, he just glared at me, waiting for me to dig the hole deeper.

I explained that I would help in other ways, and that if he had difficulty with my decision, that perhaps we should both go talk to the principal – a reasonable guy – and discuss it. More glaring. I slowly walked up and placed the ticket books on the edge of his desk. Freeman jumped up, chair falling over – another intimidation tactic – and proceeded to tell me that I better pick up those tickets if I knew what was good for me. An indescribable fear clutched at me as I slowly returned to my desk. Freeman said that we would discuss this *after* class, and everyone in the room knew what that meant.

As the bell rings, everyone clears out of the room faster than the townsfolk in a B Western when the bad guy comes to town. Freeman glares at me and then…slowly smiles. "Go on," he says. "Go to California."

Looking back on it now, I realize that it was my first real 'moment of principle,' where my integrity was put to the test on an issue of fairness.

For all my struggles with algebra that year, I remember squeaking by with a D+. Math was not my gift. English was.

The following year, due to some last minute changes, Freeman was assigned to teach my English literature class. "This *can't* be happening! Not two years in a row!" But the gods must've been smiling on me. The difference between algebra and literature came down to this: there was only *one* correct answer in algebra; English literature is *all* interpretation.

That difference worked in my favor as I spent the next three months "interpreting" rings around Freeman. On the rare occasion that he would challenge an answer, I would reiterate my line of reasoning, quoting any supportive material, then finish by pointing out that, of course, this was my interpretation. It got to the point where Freeman would call on *me* to explain to others the various metaphors and meanings of stories, poems and plays. I think Freeman respected my opinion because he knew that I wasn't trying to bluff him with bullshit. And I must say, I enjoyed this little taste of respect. I wish I could say that I lived up to that respect.

One day, he called a pop-quiz. It represented all of five points toward our total grade, but it was Freeman's way of keeping everyone on their toes in keeping up with the reading assignments.

This was not a problem for me, but the guy sitting across from me was. Mr. Bad News had made it clear, on more than one occasion, that anyone who comes from California was one step up from a cockroach. When Freeman announced that we would exchange papers with our neighbor, a hand reached across the aisle, grabbed mine, and said that we would *not* be switching papers. "Understand?"

I had a quick decision to make: take a chance on getting caught cheating by Freeman or be assured of a reckoning with Bad News. We didn't exchange papers, but I told my "neighbor" to allow for at least one incorrect answer so it wouldn't look obvious. After going over the answers, Freeman is calling the roll, asking everyone their grade. Bad News confidently yells out, "100%!"

"What!" Freeman says, as he leaps from his chair and begins to approach the two of us.

"Who graded your paper?"

"Lichtman, sir."

"Lichtman! Well, that's different." Without a pause, Freeman turns and heads back to his desk.

Although I felt bad at the time, I had rationalized to myself that it was just a five-point quiz. What difference would it possibly make?

A month later, after telling a few friends that I would be moving back to California at the end of the semester, Freeman, uncharacteristically announced it to the entire class along with one thing more: "Lichtman is the only one in this class who has stood up to me. He's the only one with any *real* class."

A five-point quiz, that's what I traded my integrity for.

Y ES, VIRGINIA, there actually *is* an Office of Government Ethics in Washington. A small agency within the executive branch, the OGE was established by the Ethics in Government Act of 1978. In partnership with executive branch agencies and departments, the OGE promotes high ethical standards for employees and strengthens the public's confidence that the government's business is conducted with impartiality and integrity. Stephen Potts – a former director – talks about the influence of a university professor and his "Integrity" test.

In 1948, Vanderbilt University's Dean of Students, Madison Sarratt, taught a freshman algebra course. On the day our class assembled for our first major exam, we found the exam questions face down on our desks. Dean Sarratt stood at ease in front of his desk. After we were seated, he said, "Today you are going to take two tests – one in algebra and one in integrity. I hope that you pass both. But if you must fail one, let it be algebra. You may now begin."

He turned and left the room. My fellow students and I briefly scanned each other and then went to work.

We all passed the integrity test. Dean Sarratt's strength of character permeated that room. I'm sure everyone shared my feeling that we had to vindicate his faith in us.

IN AN EARLIER STATEMENT, former baseball pitcher John McCarthy described a litany of courtesies and kindnesses that he stands for. McCarthy's philosophy may sound simplistic, but his convictions are not immune to the challenges of success when it comes to his Elementary Baseball program and a moment of integrity.

One of my strongest beliefs is that something is not an ideal until it costs you something. I have heard that sentiment said before, and I had an opportunity to put it into practice a few years ago.

The place was an elementary school in Washington, D.C. where I am the director of an after-school reading and baseball program for forty boys and girls ages six through twelve. The school is located in Washington's

Shaw neighborhood. Over 95% live below the poverty level, and the majority does not have a father at home. The program features one-on-one reading tutoring with a volunteer high-school student, and one-on-one mentoring from a D.C. Superior Court Judge. If the students hit the books as hard as the fastball down the middle, they'll play on the team in the spring. The program was chosen by the U.S. Justice Department as the nation's top urban after-school program on the elementary level.

My chance to practice my ideal came out of the blue when I was invited to the principal's office and was met by producers from a network news magazine. The pitch was to have a prominent American citizen visit the Elementary Baseball program followed by cameras – the message being that more Americans ought to get involved in such programs. I was told that the network program would air to over ten million viewers. The principal and the producer told me what a great opportunity it was for the school, the children and my program. Specifically, he requested I call the chief judge of D.C. Superior Court and ask him if he could come down the next day so they could film him interacting with the children at practice as the prominent individual did a walkthrough.

I told him I needed several hours to think about this. After speaking with the chief judge and several people whose opinions I trust, I came back with a polite, but firm, no. I told the principal and the producers my reasons were simple. First, I thought the story of Elementary Baseball and its tutors and mentors was a worthy story on its own.

Second, I felt like the notable was being a swooper – one, who shows up with the camera, expands on the virtues of citizen involvement, only to never be seen again.

I was told that I wasn't being a "team player" and I was depriving "the children" and my program of a chance for national exposure. The producer even offered to include our address on air where viewers could send a donation to Elementary Baseball. I spent the next two hours in the principal's office being stroked, nudged and browbeaten. I held my ground and told the producer that if he ever wants to do a story on EB, I'd be more than happy to be a part of it, but I would not be a part of a network swoop that uses EB students as props to polish the image of a prominent individual until his next gig comes along.

Post Script: The principal moved on a year later to another position. The chief judge who wholeheartedly agreed with my position, retired two years later and still serves as a mentor to the program. And Elementary Baseball is still chugging along doing small things in great ways.

CARL PRUDE has been involved in several sales positions throughout his career. His story is not an unusual one, but it makes clear that nothing can take the place of a reputation for doing what's right and the necessary integrity in placing principle over expediency.

My story took place in the early days of my sales career. Our sales team was on the verge of winning a contest against two other sales teams. The prize was a three-day weekend for the entire winning team and their spouses at the Red Lion Resort in Santa Barbara. Our team was about $50,000 behind the leading team, and we had come to the final day of the contest. At about 4:30 p.m. I received a call from a customer regarding a proposal I had given him about three months prior.

After discussing some changes he wanted in the design, and some price wrangling, the customer gave me a verbal commitment to a $47,000 contract. Another sales person had just walked in with a $10,000 contract, so my contract would put our team over the top. There was one catch, however. In order for the sale to count towards the contest, a signed contract had to be faxed into our corporate order entry department. I only had a verbal commitment from this customer. When I discovered I needed a signed contract, I called his office but was told that he had left for the weekend. Furthermore, his secretary said that he was the only one who could sign our contract.

I told my manager about the situation, and he told me to go copy the original contract, sign the customer's name to the copy, and fax it into the corporate office. My boss rationalized that since the customer had given us a verbal agreement, he was going to sign the contract on Monday anyway. I balked at the idea of forging someone else's name, and I kindly refused to do it. At this point my boss became visibly upset; he stormed into his office, slamming the door behind him. After about 15 minutes he called me into his office and explained to me how things happen sometimes in the "real business world." My response was that if he wanted the contract signed that badly, that he should sign it himself. The day ended with him upset with me and the contract left in its virgin state.

The following Monday, the customer called and said that he would have to delay signing the contract until it was reviewed by his board of directors. This took about 45 days, so it was really a good thing that I hadn't listened to my boss. Subsequently, our team ended up winning the trip because a large sale that was turned in by one of the other sales teams ended up being turned down because the customer couldn't get credit approved.

The principle I followed was just being honest and doing business with integrity. My experience has been that there are more honest people in the business world than those who fall into the category of less than honest. When it's time to hit the pillow, there's no substitute for a clear conscience, or for a good reputation in the office.

FORMER NEW JERSEY GOVERNOR and Environmental Protection Agency Administrator Christie Whitman's 'moment' occurred "…literally hours after I was elected governor in 1993."

The principle that guides my life is the importance of maintaining my personal integrity, no matter what. No goal, no gain, no achievement is worth compromising one's honesty and integrity. I learned this from my parents. I remember vividly my father once explaining to me why he wouldn't deduct from his taxes the depreciation for his farm equipment. He didn't agree with the policy of depreciation, so he wasn't going to take the tax break it offered. Whenever I'm confronted with a challenge to my own sense of personal integrity, I ask myself, "is this something I could explain to my children and still merit their respect?" That always helps make things quite clear.

Governor Whitman offered this personal account taken from a commencement address she gave at Colgate University in Hamilton, New York on May 18, 1997.

"Perhaps the biggest challenge my moral compass ever faced occurred literally hours after I was elected governor in 1993.

"Two days after the election, our campaign's most prominent strategist went to a breakfast meeting with a roomful of reporters. For reasons that I will never understand, he told those reporters that the key to my victory was his brilliant effort to suppress the voter turnout among urban blacks by, in effect, bribing African-American religious leaders in those communities.

"Until I draw my last breath, I will remember how the news of this outrageous lie knocked the wind out of me. I knew – for a certainty – that our campaign wouldn't have done this. It was simply inconceivable. I quickly confirmed my belief by talking to those involved in my campaign – including our so-called strategic genius. Everyone assured me that my campaign had done no such thing.

What Do You Stand For?

"Our strong denials, however, did nothing to extinguish the firestorm that erupted. Understandably, the media, our opponents, and the state's black clergy members wanted a full investigation. Not only did this story impugn the integrity of my campaign, it also smeared the reputations of those religious leaders who stood accused of accepting bribes for keeping down the vote in their communities.

"I knew I had to act quickly – not so much to secure my victory but to restore my integrity. Some suggested that I brand the calls for an investigation as nothing more than a partisan effort to reverse the election. Others maintained that I should move forward with putting my administration together, ignoring the serious questions that had been raised. My own moral compass, however, was pointing in another direction.

"I decided that there was only one honorable course to take. I had to announce that I would delay my inauguration so long as there was any credible evidence that my campaign subverted the electoral process. I could not – and would not – assume office under the cloud that we had somehow stolen the election.

"I always believed that it wasn't healthy to spend too much time reveling in the thrill of victory. But take my word for it; there must be better ways to come back down to earth. It wasn't easy to voluntarily offer up my victory as the price to pay if these charges proved to be true. But it was the right thing to do.

"The weeks that followed were filled with the most extensive electoral investigation ever conducted in the

State of New Jersey. Not a single piece of evidence was ever found to support the charge that we had bribed our way to victory. That's because we hadn't.

"This was one case in which the truth of Harper Lee's observation in *To Kill a Mockingbird* was literally true. 'The one thing that doesn't abide by majority rule is a person's conscience.' The hundreds of thousands of votes I had received would not have been enough to defeat the single vote my conscience had cast."

TONY HAWK, described as "the most famous alternative athlete of his time," is 33 years old, and a father of three. He has been skateboarding since he was 9. Hawk learned to skate at a time when the California landscape was dotted with skateparks. The Tony Hawk Foundation was created for the express purpose of funding more skateparks throughout the country, to encourage kids in pursuing the self-esteem they get from perfecting a move, defying gravity. His account shows how important it is for celebrities to set a positive example.

I stand for equality, integrity, perseverance, and making your dreams a reality.

I once received a lucrative offer to do a skating tour through a country that I have never visited, which was very enticing. However, the title sponsor for this tour was a tobacco manufacturer. Although cigarette smoking is very common in this particular country, there is no way I could justify promoting this company. I feel like I maintained a level of integrity by choosing not to endorse a tobacco manufacturer, and I can only hope that my lack of involvement discouraged kids from smoking in some way.

In April 1998, for the first time in our nation's history, the director of the United States Secret Service was asked to testify against a sitting president in court. Independent counsel Kenneth Starr wanted to question Lewis Merletti about Bill Clinton's meetings with Monica Lewinsky. Starr was trying to find out whether the president lied under oath when he denied a sexual relationship with Lewinsky to Paula Jones' lawyers.

In a declaration made in opposition to Starr's Motion to Compel testimony from Secret Service agents, Merletti argued that agents could refuse to testify because they are shielded by a "protective envelope" privilege similar to those covering doctors, lawyers and clergy. (The privilege, it was pointed out, did not extend to any area that covered an agent witnessing the commission of a crime.)

At the core of Merletti's statement to Starr was this passionate defense of trust:

> "The history of the Secret Service provides a strong foundation for this tradition of unequivocal trust. The motto of the United States Secret Service is 'WORTHY OF TRUST AND CONFIDENCE.' This tenet is so central to our mission it is emblazoned in the Secret Service Commission Book. I feel so strongly about this creed that when I speak to agents upon their graduation, I tell them that the 'most important' factor

in the Secret Service Commission Book is the one in which 'I commend you to the entire world as being worthy of TRUST and CONFIDENCE.' As I state, the phrase, 'BEING WORTHY OF TRUST AND CONFIDENCE' is the absolute heart and soul of the United States Secret Service. This trust and confidence cannot be situational. It cannot have an expiration date. And it must never be compromised."

My life lessons go back to 1967 with my enlistment in the United States Army. At the age of 19, I completed basic training, advanced infantry training, and jump school. I was recruited into the Army's Special Forces Training Group. There I completed one year of Special Forces qualification courses, then on to Vietnamese language school. During my tour of duty in Vietnam, I learned many things. It was my first exposure to leading people in a stressful, often hostile environment. I experienced cultural diversity. Our Special Forces team consisted of whites, blacks, Hispanics, and American Indians. We depended on each other, we trusted each other, we cared about each other, we were a team. We worked alongside the Montagnards, Cambodians, and Vietnamese, and we were a team. We lived their culture and learned not to impose ours upon them. We were accepted by them and our mission succeeded.

Those lessons became the foundation for the principles that guided me throughout my career in the United States Secret Service, an agency composed of highly dedicated men and women.

As I rose through the ranks, ultimately becoming the

19th Director of the United States Secret Service, I developed a reputation of team building, vision and forward thinking. During my tenure as director, the Secret Service experienced one of its most critical tests. That test came in the form of the Office of the Independent Counsel's request for Secret Service testimony. Never in the history of our agency had we been asked to violate our standard of trust and confidence.

For the Secret Service the issue of trust and confidence was decidedly non-partisan and non-political; the training and activities of U.S.S.S. personnel transcend political party or the crisis of the moment. We live according to an unwritten code, an invisible web of obligation; we would sooner die than fail.

The decision I made, however, was not made in a vacuum. Although I had a strong sense of what the Service's position should be, I sought the counsel of all four living former directors. I also sought the opinions of all the living former Special Agents in Charge of the Presidential Protective Division. When I asked what they would do, to a man they answered, "trust and confidentiality *is* what this Agency has always stood for. You're the first to be tested. You have no option; you must stand firm on this agency's strong heritage and tradition. Don't let us down."

I firmly believe that history will record our stance as one that was prudent, well planned, and required for the survival of our Agency's reputation and its ability to successfully carry out its critical National Security mission.

I wish to share the following creed, origin unknown,

which I have carried for over 30 years. I consider it to be a touchstone that has inspired me during the most trying times.

"To bear up under loss, to fight the bitterness of defeat and the weakness of grief, to be victor over anger, to smile when tears are close, to resist evil men and base instincts, to hate hate and to love love, to go on when it would seem good to die, to seek ever after the glory and the dream, to look up with unquenchable faith in something evermore about to be. To maintain dignity and integrity, surrender is not in this creed. This is what any man can do and so be great."

Based on his testimony and support of lawyers from the Justice and Treasury departments, the "Trust and Confidence" standard of the Secret Service was upheld. Lewis Merletti retired from the Secret Service on January 2, 1999. He currently serves as Executive Vice President, Stadium and Security for the Cleveland Browns football team.

N EWSWEEK WRITER and senior editor Jonathan Alter's response to my questionnaire reflects on the influence of an Illinois governor.

I'm inspired by the story of Peter Altgeld, governor of Illinois a century ago. Altgeld sacrificed his political career to do the right thing in the case of the Haymarket Riot. In 1886, anarchists held a rally in Chicago. As police advanced to break up the crowd, a bomb was tossed and seven policemen were killed. Because the authorities couldn't figure out who threw the bomb, they decided to arrest the eight most prominent anarchists in town on the theory that their ideas contributed to the carnage, even though several were not even present that day. The trial was a travesty of justice, with no evidence and several jurors publicly proclaiming the guilt of the defendants. The anti-labor fever of the time created intense public opinion against the anarchists that lasted on into the 1890's, when Altgeld became governor.

Altgeld had a big future in politics, but when the Haymarket case reached his desk in 1893, he pardoned the three surviving anarchists. When his secretary of state asked him why he insisted on the pardons, Altgeld pounded on the desk with his fist and answered with three words: "It is right." Altgeld lost his bid for re-election, left office broke and died a few years later.

I didn't think of Altgeld directly when I wrote in *Newsweek* about the importance of making sure death row inmates are given their proper DNA tests (our story led then-Governor Bush to issue his first-ever stay of execution), but his example – and quest for justice – clearly influenced me.

JOE PHELPS is one of the pioneering innovators of integrated marketing communications, which combines advertising, public relations, and promotions into a consistent marketing campaign. The Phelps Group's success is due to Phelps' ongoing commitment to a mission statement that clearly defines what they expect from both the agency and its clients. In part, it reads:

"Our mission…is to do great work for deserving clients, in a healthy working environment, to realize our clients' goals and our potentials."

We define "deserving" as those clients whose products make the world a better place to live – and who treat us like human beings.

When we were about $14 million in billings, a friend came to me and offered to bring in a large account ($12 million) but said there were some strings attached. He said the account would be extremely profitable, but the client had a severe drinking problem, which invariably results in agency people working very hard, but never seeing the results of their labor. He also said that we'd sometimes have to lie about the client's whereabouts.

This account represented a lot of money for us. It would virtually double the agency's size. I thought about it for a couple of days. On one hand, I wanted the revenue; on the other, I didn't want to destroy the harmony of our young, but fast-growing and very healthy agency.

Here's how I solved the dilemma. I basically went into the future and looked back to the present.

Our growth plans called for 25% growth per year. I could see on the chart that it wouldn't be very many years until we would reach $50 million in billings. And I knew that if we maintained our present course, we would get there, and be a well-rounded company working for

WHAT DO YOU STAND FOR?

"deserving clients," and would be proud of our accomplishments. However, if we took this big, but troublesome account, it could ruin our healthy environment, and we might never realize our real goals. So, the decision was easy. We turned down the account and have always been glad we did. This year our billings will be $44 million, and we will probably reach $50 million before the end of next year.

If you're ever having trouble making a big decision, mentally go into the future and look back to the present. Things can get crystal clear from that vantage point.

LINDA CHAVEZ has held a number of political positions, among them White House Director of Public Liaison, Staff Director of the U.S. Commission on Civil Rights as well as U.S. expert to the United Nations Sub-commission on the Prevention of Discrimination and Protection of Minorities. She currently serves as president of the Center for Equal Opportunity. When faced with taking legal advantage of a program that she disagreed with politically but that would help her son, Chavez chose to stand on principle.

For my entire professional career I have championed the principle that each person should be judged on his or her own merit, without regard to color or sex. In the early years of the modern civil-rights movement, this principle enjoyed wide support. Indeed, our civil-rights laws are based on the idea that it is wrong to discriminate against anyone because of race, national origin, or sex. But in recent years, our nation's commitment to colorblind justice appears to have eroded. In fact, some people now argue that the only way to make up for past discrimination is to give preferential treatment to members of groups that had been unfairly treated in the past.

I grew up at a time when there was considerable discrimination against blacks, Hispanics, women, and others. I certainly faced my share of unpleasant experiences based on my ethnicity. I was called names, forced off playgrounds, even denied a job once because the man doing the hiring didn't believe that I had actually written the published work I submitted. Nonetheless, it has never made sense to me that I should now be given preferential treatment to make up for the past. It makes even less sense that my children – who faced very little discrimination or prejudice in their own lives – should suddenly benefit from affirmative action programs or racial preferences.

When my oldest son applied for college, our family had the chance to test these principles. Several schools offering scholarships for Hispanic students tried to recruit my son. After long discussions at the dinner table, we decided not to apply for these race-based programs, even though they would have saved our family thousands of dollars.

The best way to end discrimination based on race or sex is simply to do just that. No one should be either advantaged or disadvantaged because of immutable characteristics over which they have no control.

WHAT DO YOU DO when you discover something wrong? What

do you do with what you know? Do you remain silent or come forward? Do you remain loyal to the company or expose the truth? And what about the impact your decision might have on your family, especially if you have a child who is in need of specialized medical attention? What do you do then?

These were some of the questions facing Dr. Jeffrey Wigand in 1995 when he decided to step forward as the highest-ranking tobacco insider and testify that Brown & Williamson and the tobacco industry not only knew that nicotine was an addictive substance, but was actively involved in manipulating nicotine levels in cigarettes. This was contrary to what the CEOs of the seven major tobacco companies had told Congress in sworn testimony in April 1994.

The cost for his integrity was high. He lost his job, his home, his wife, and for a time, his reputation.

In the months and years that followed, Wigand's story has been told in a variety of forms including the feature film, *The Insider*. However, his own in-depth account gives us a greater sense of what he was truly up against. It's a story about honesty over loyalty; duty over deceit; persistence over pressure. What we come away with is not only a scientist's search for the truth, but the moral courage necessary to reveal that truth in spite of the consequences to himself.

Although we may never face the kind of test of our integrity Jeff Wigand faced, at some time most of us will face choices involving honesty, loyalty, duty, and the necessary courage to make the right call.

My moral compass has an intolerance for deceit. It's a

compass that makes me want to make sure that the truth is told, particularly when it affects the health and safety of millions of people.

I arrived at Brown & Williamson in December of 1988 and began work on the development of an engineered tobacco product that reduces the risk of lung cancer, emphysema, chronic obstructive pulmonary disease, or heart disease. I was recruited by B&W after twenty-five years of senior management experience with the healthcare industry working for companies such as Pfizer, Merck, and Johnson & Johnson. I was steeped in a mindset of using science to search for the truth, to make products better, to improve the quality of life and to save lives.

My first experience shortly after joining the company was to be sent to the law firm of Shook, Hardy and Bacon outside of Kansas City, Missouri. It was my first encounter with how entrenched the lawyers were in the manipulation of the science of smoking and health. I spent three days being asked to believe that the numerous U.S. Surgeon-General's reports were all based on flawed science and that the conclusions of Sir Richard Doll, the late Dr. Oscar Auerbach, and many others were just plain wrong. This was the first time I ever had lawyers interpret the science of tobacco and health for me.

I understood why this was happening. For decades, the industry has survived on two basic tenets: First, that there is no causal relationship between tobacco use and illnesses associated with tobacco addiction; and second, that nicotine is not addictive – for if there was an admission that

WHAT DO YOU STAND FOR?

nicotine was addictive, the free-choice position would be moot. I returned to my corporate headquarters confused but not deterred from developing a safer product.

In September of 1989, I was part of a Research Policy Group (RPG) meeting where all the senior managers of research and development from British-American Tobacco, the parent company of Brown & Williamson and BAT-affiliated companies, had gathered to develop strategic research priorities and programs. For four and a half days, we discussed, among other things, how to make a safer product.

This extensive meeting generated over twelve pages of detailed notes memorializing the scientific discussions and a follow-up action program to achieve the strategic goals – a biologically safer tobacco product, a fire-safe cigarette, and so forth. We clearly articulated the company's internal mantra: *"We are in the nicotine-delivery business, and tar is the negative baggage."* In other words, nicotine is addictive and pharmacologically active, and there could be a product that was safer but never safe.

When the minutes of this meeting reached the senior executives of the company, they were clearly distressed, for we had thus articulated the antithesis of the mantra meant for the public: *"Nicotine is there for taste and is not addictive; tobacco products can be made safer in many ways, from less biologically active to fire-safe."* I was unprepared for what happened next, even after twenty-five years of senior management experience.

The president and chief operating officer of the company, Mr. Thomas Sandefur, with the agreement of the chief executive officer/chairman Ray Pritchard, ordered an attorney, J. Kendrick Wells III, to rewrite the minutes. Mr. Wells rewrote the minutes so that there would be no document within the company records that would refute the prevailing external science or to be at odds with the company's deliberate obfuscation relating to nicotine's addictive nature and smoking-and-health issues. Mr. Wells had not attended the RPG meeting, but he vetted the minutes from twelve pages to two-and-a-half pages by including only the follow-up program and removing any reference to what actually happened. The specific purpose was to prevent the discovery of a document that could undermine decades of not telling the truth, in both legal and public statements. Clearly unethical. What followed next was just as egregious if not more alarming.

At the direction of BAT CEO/Chairman Sir Patrick Sheehey, a lawyer would be placed in every sequence of scientific communication and research. A system of sequestering and vetting controversial documents generated by any of the operating companies was ordered. In addition, all safer-cigarette work was terminated and all further work on that project was transferred overseas, along with the documents; for if there were a safer tobacco product, all other products would be deemed unsafe.

Now I was in a quandary as to what I do with what I knew.

I had a wife, two young children, one with a medical issue from birth requiring extensive medical coverage, a mortgage, a car, a $300,000-a year salary, and all the amenities of a successful executive. I was also keenly aware by now of how the industry intimidated defectors, paying legions of lawyers to attack their credibility in an effort to stop their behavior. I wanted no part of that and wanted to protect my family and to reengineer a transition back to the healthcare industry; for now I realized I had made a major error in my career.

Subsequently, I found myself turning to investigate health issues relating to the use of tobacco products, including the role played by additives and cigarette design on nicotine deliveries, marketing to adolescents, and the premature death caused by tobacco products. I also observed how the industry used science to generate controversy rather than using science to search for the truth.

The more I learned, the more I had difficulty looking in the mirror. I wondered how I would continue to explain to my two young children why I worked for the tobacco industry. I did my best not to rock the boat until August of 1992, when I received a draft copy of a National Toxicology Program report exposing *coumarin*, one of the additives used by the company, as carcinogenic.

The industry nurtures the belief that a tobacco product is a natural product, grown in the ground and wrapped in paper. This is far from the truth. Tobacco products are laced with over 599 intentionally added chemical additives that are put into the tobacco and waste tobacco-derived materials in order to ameliorate the harshness generated when burning a bioorganic material. This bioorganic material, tobacco, generates over 5,000 toxic chemical pyrolysis compounds. These combustion chemicals are so toxic you cannot bury them in solid-waste disposal areas. These additives mask the acridity of nicotine as well as the irritation of smoke. They also facilitate the efficient delivery of an addictive substance.

In 1984, the FDA took coumarin off its GRAS list (Generally Recognized As Safe). Subsequently, the industry was not only forced to remove it from all of its cigarette products, but is also required to report any and all additives in cigarettes to Congress, annually. However, in spite of the obvious health risks, Brown & Williamson continued to use coumarin in pipe tobacco.

When I went to Mr. Sandefur in the fall of 1992 with this knowledge that coumarin tests as a lung-specific carcinogen, he instructed me to go back to the lab. Unless I found a substitute, he was not going to allow coumarin to be taken out of the product because its removal would affect the taste of the pipe, and this would negatively affect sales and profits. Sandefur's reasoning: if we are not legally barred, we'll continue to use it.

Coumarin was not removed from the pipe-tobacco formulation even though there was substantial, new scientific information that could put the pipe-tobacco user at an incremental health risk. This final issue caused me to be fired in March of 1993, when Mr. Sandefur became the new chief executive officer. At the time I left the company, coumarin was still used in the formulation of the Sir Walter Raleigh pipe-tobacco product.

When I was terminated, all I wanted was to forget

four years and three months of a bad mistake and go back to where I belonged – the healthcare industry. In June of 1993, a negotiated severance package with two years' salary continuation and the all-important health coverage for my daughter was executed. The company also agreed to remove other restrictions that they had initially required: I could now take my knowledge to work for another tobacco company if I chose to do so, for example, and there was no longer a severance salary offset for early employment.

In September of 1993, the company sued me in a Kentucky court for allegedly violating my severance agreement by telling another employee my annual salary. With the filing of the lawsuit, they immediately interrupted my severance pay and health coverage. However, they offered me the opportunity to drop the lawsuit and reinstate what I had already contracted for by signing a new more draconian secrecy agreement – one which would prevent me, without their direct legal involvement, from ever discussing with anyone anything I knew of the internal workings of the company unless there was a legal instrument that required me to discuss and/or testify to what I knew, learned or observed while in the employ of the company. This offer was coincident with the first of two U.S. Department of Justice civil investigative demands, a kind of federal subpoena, on fire-safe cigarettes, which I received in December of 1993.

I signed the newly extorted agreement; the lawsuit was dropped, and my previously negotiated healthcare and the severance package was reinstated, but now labored with an onerous confidentiality agreement.

In January 1994, I served as a technical consultant to CBS *60 Minutes* for the program, "Up in Smoke" that aired in April of that year. Mr. Lowell Bergman, a producer with 60 Minutes, had been the recipient of an anonymous set of confidential internal tobacco industry documents from Philip Morris, the world's largest producer of tobacco products.

The documents described a natural incendiary product that had a reduced fire-generating capacity and tested the same as their leading brand: it looked the same, tasted the same, cost the same. It had no incremental toxicity as their leading brand. However, Philip Morris chose not to introduce the product because there were no regulatory requirements to do so even though a reduced-ignition-propensity had the potential of saving 1,200 to 1,500 lives attributed to fires created by cigarettes. They named it *Hamlet*..."to burn or not to burn."

What was more disconcerting was that as a B&W executive, I sat across from these Philip Morris' representatives during several joint venture meetings and listened as they repeatedly asserted that the development of a reduced-ignition-propensity cigarette was an impossibility. My knowledge of this company's relentless duplicity bothered me considerably.

In February of 1994, then commissioner of the FDA, Dr. David Kessler, began the process of establishing regulatory authority over tobacco and nicotine as an addictive substance. In addition, the U.S. Congress initiated its inquiry into tobacco issues. In the process of developing their information-gathering they contacted me to see if I was willing to help Congress in its investigation.

I was willing to be of assistance, but I informed them that I had a very onerous secrecy agreement and that if I were to help them, I would have to be served with a Congressional subpoena. Because my agreement with B&W was so restrictive and because I needed to protect my family from the loss of severance salary and health benefits, I reported to B&W that I had been contacted by the U.S. Congress regarding my knowledge of tobacco chemistry, cigarette design, and so forth.

What followed changed the course of all future actions and as a practical matter changed our family. I was warned that if I spoke to anyone regarding the internal workings of Brown & Williamson, my two young daughters would be harmed. I immediately made the connection between my reporting and the threats. I went to the local Federal Bureau of Investigation. A "trap and trace" was installed on my phone line and two threats made by phone were isolated. From that day forward I never told Brown & Williamson my activities nor any of my contacts pertinent to tobacco matters. As a practical matter, it did not matter where the threats came from, they changed our environment permanently.

In April of 1994, the seven chief executive officers of all the major U.S. tobacco companies, including my former boss Mr. Sandefur, appeared in the U.S, Congress under oath. They stated that nicotine was *not* addictive and that it was there for taste and that smoking was no more dangerous to your health than eating Twinkies.

As that indelible image replayed itself in my mind, I realized that by my silence I was no different from the men on my television screen. I then chose to do something very different with my knowledge about tobacco chemistry, additives, genetically engineered tobacco, impact boosting with ammonia-based additives, smoke chemistry – the keys to the understanding of tobacco products.

I began to share my knowledge with the FDA. I did it with the agreement that I would have a completely anonymous working relationship. My code name in the FDA was "Research," something right out of a James Bond novel. The FDA realized that its investigation threatened the tobacco industry. The FDA also knew that the industry would do anything to derail this investigation.

In the summer of 1995, a professor of cardiology at the University of California at San Francisco, Dr. Stanton Glantz, contacted me. Dr. Glantz was the recipient of tobacco documents smuggled out of Brown & Williamson. (These documents are the subject of seven *Journal of the American Medical Association* articles and a book, *The Cigarette Papers*.) Dr. Glantz shared these 1950-through-1980s documents with me in the process of writing these manuscripts. These documents mirrored my exact experiences from 1989 through 1993 at B&W as they also provided me the first opportunity to see data I never saw while at B&W.

This was the final and culminating step in my journey

to an epiphany. I would reveal the truth about the tobacco industry: its disregard for public health and safety, its use of additives to boost nicotine's addictiveness, and its lawyers' obfuscation of the truth and their intimate involvement in science and document destruction. Of course, this information contradicted Mr. Sandefur's Congressional testimony and his daily remarks in his office. I felt a higher obligation to public health and safety and to the truth than to an onerous agreement that intended to deliberately hide the truth through intimidation and extortion.

On August 5, 1995, I elected to share my knowledge with the public via CBS *60 Minutes*. I needed to set my moral compass back on a true heading. I gave the interview with the full cooperation of my family and they actively participated in the interview. However, I did not give the interview without some caveats: I would maintain custody and control of the taped interview until such time as: 1) I had competent legal representation; 2) had my house in order; and 3) CBS arranged for physical security once the show had aired. I knew full well that I would need a good lawyer and I wanted to make sure my children were not harmed in any way.

In the early fall of 1995, many things were happening at CBS: Westinghouse had tendered an acquisition offer to buy CBS; Lawrence Tisch and his brother Robert were principal owners of CBS via Loews Corporation, which also owns Lorillard Tobacco Company; Lawrence Tisch's son Andrew, the chairman of Lorillard, was among the seven CEOs who testified in front of Congress in April of

1994, testimony being investigated for perjury by the U.S. Department of Justice. To make things more dicey, B&W and Lorillard were negotiating a $100 million tobacco product acquisition.

The common denominator for all these complex issues was that the lawyers at CBS were also assessing the airing of my interview with Mike Wallace and *60 Minutes* and the legal principle of *tortious interference* – the causing of harm by disrupting something that belongs to someone else.

Somehow Brown & Williamson learned of the interview and threatened CBS with a lawsuit for billions in damages if it aired the interview. This suit would reflect negatively on the balance sheet of CBS during the acquisition. CBS management and its legal department canned the program as a result of this legal threat and succumbed to the threats of the tobacco industry. Instead of airing the original interview, CBS aired a muted edition of the original program.

In October, someone within CBS leaked the complete interview to the New York media. Bedlam hit Louisville when the story hit the streets. I was sued again, this time for theft of trade secrets and violation of my confidentiality agreement. I was restrained from discussing tobacco. CBS, through Mr. Bergman, provided us with round-the-clock physical security by armed, former secret service agents. They lived with us every minute, checked and opened the daily mail, started the car in the morning, followed me to my job, where I taught high school chemistry, biology, physical sciences, and Japanese. They checked my classroom, escorted my two daughters to school, to play, and so forth. Ultimately, the school was forced to place physical security at my classroom door due to the recurrent daily threats. Not a fun time.

Shortly before this, I was afforded access to an excellent attorney from Mississippi by the name of Dickie Scruggs. He offered his legal services to me *pro bono* and after meeting him, I accepted his generosity. Mr. Scruggs was affluent of heart and resources, and he was committed to protecting me in my search for the truth.

In November, I was served my second subpoena from the U.S. Department of Justice on fire-safe cigarettes. I was also served by the state of Mississippi for their civil suit against the tobacco industry for recovering healthcare costs from decades of treating adult smokers who became sick as a result of becoming addicted as children. I traveled to Mississippi and stayed at Mr. Scruggs' home so that I would be in a secure environment before the depositions. Dickie's home had to be swept for an electronic eavesdropping device before we stayed there, and armed Mississippi State Police patrolled it all night.

When I finished the morning deposition, I returned to Mr. Scruggs' home for lunch and a new development. I was told by Dickie, attorney-general Mike Moore, and attorney, Ron Motley, that if I went forward in the afternoon with the civil deposition, I would face going to jail for contempt in Kentucky. Brown & Williamson had obtained a temporary restraining order (a gag order) from a Kentucky court. My decision whether or not to give the deposition was a big one, but all three attorneys assured me that they would stay with me no matter which decision I made.

I needed time to think. I wandered the lawn in front of Dickie's home searching for the right thing to do. I did not want to go to jail in Kentucky for telling the truth under oath, the same information I provided CBS voluntarily in August.

After reflecting on the issues, I decided to go forward with the deposition. After all, I had already paid the price, and if I did not go forward, then I would most likely never get the opportunity to do it again. B&W would tie me up in court indefinitely.

I have never looked back since that day. The tobacco industry lawyers were as abundant as sand on the beach and adamant in their efforts to prevent the deposition with threats and constant verbal interruptions. Mr. Motley took charge of this courtroom and succeeded in getting the right information in the record under oath. It was the first time I think the overpowering tobacco industry lawyers found their match. My testimony was sealed. I returned to Kentucky and was met by U.S. Marshals arranged by Mississippi Attorney-General Mike Moore and the Department of Justice. I did not go to jail that night. I went home and went to teach school the next day.

January of 1996 was the beginning of the turning point for many things in this tobacco war. The sealed deposition from Mississippi found its way to the *Wall Street Journal*. Under the threat of a lawsuit by Brown &

What Do You Stand For?

Williamson, that paper not only published the full deposition on the front page but also loaded it up on the Internet. B&W was beside itself. Their threat did not work as it had worked twice before.

B&W then spent what must have been millions for a smear campaign with private investigators, a publicist, and large law firms. But it did not succeed in discrediting me in the court of public opinion because the *Wall Street Journal* refused to print a story without assessing the validity of the accusations. The local paper in Louisville, on the other hand, published the B&W orchestrated smear without investigating any of the allegations. And to add more fuel to the fire, someone – even with two armed security personnel – managed to put a live bullet in my mailbox with another threat directed at my daughters.

The month culminated with a divorce notification from my wife on the exact date of our tenth wedding anniversary. That is the most disappointing aspect of my whole journey.

Some people ask, given the personal and professional consequences of my decision to come forward with what I knew, would I do it again? In a heartbeat. I have no rancor or regrets. I did what I thought was right and would do it again. Each of us should realize that we can make a difference.

In June 1997, thirty-nine states' attorneys-general concluded a $368 billion dollar settlement with the tobacco industry as a result of Dr. Wigand's testimony. However, Brown & Williamson refused to drop their lawsuit against him. It was only after *ALL* thirty-nine attorneys-general threatened to walk out on settlement negotiations and continue individual lawsuits in each state that British-American Tobacco new head Martin Broughton reluctantly agreed to end the suit.

Currently, Jeff Wigand travels throughout the United States and the world speaking to kids and groups of all ages regarding the truth about smoking. For more information about his program Smoke-Free Kids, contact jeffreywigand.com.

FRANK SESNO was a familiar face and voice at CNN for 17 years, from the White House to the anchor set. For nearly seven years, Sesno served as CNN's White House correspondent. From 1996 through 2001 he was Senior Vice President and Washington Bureau Chief, responsible for the network's largest bureau and coverage decisions at the White House, Congress, the Pentagon, and State and Justice Departments as well as general assignment reporting.

As a journalist, Sesno has reported on events ranging from the wars of Central America to the release of America's hostages in Iran; from the Middle East Peace talks to the impeachment and trial of President Bill Clinton; from the election of 2000 to the terror attacks of September 11, 2001. He has interviewed world leaders ranging from Presidents Bill Clinton, George Bush, and Ronald Reagan to Egyptian President Hosni Mubarak, former Israeli Prime Minister Benjamin Netanyahu, and Jordan's King Hussein. Sesno's response raises an important question of integrity when it comes to balance between work and family.

After 17 years on the front lines of history, in one of the

most interesting jobs on the planet, I decided to leave CNN. I had concluded it was time to move in new directions, to drill down deeper into the issues that shape our world, to teach in new ways. I was seeing things I didn't like in commercial television: more focus on ratings, more attention to the bottom line, more emphasis on personality and pizzazz. The desperate drive for audience retention – 'eyeballs' – was increasingly pushing us toward production and personality rather than news and content. In the end, the first priority of news should be to inform – with fairness, accuracy, balance, and hard thought about what matters.

On another, very personal level, the time had come to reinvest in my family. At work, at home, and in the community, I have always tried to encourage and pursue honesty, fairness, credibility, curiosity and integrity. These are the enduring values that have governed my journalistic mission. And they have been the benchmarks for my family, as I teach my children to be true to their word, respect the people and the world around them, and ask 'why' as often as they can.

But asking questions can be unsettling. Asking questions of ourselves can lead to the most unexpected answers of all. The answers may not be what we or others expect. Sometimes we are confronted with tough choices we'd rather avoid or have someone else make for us. But the process can lead to understanding and action.

A constant question for me has always revolved around the issue of balance. Balance in the presentation of viewpoints. Balance in a story well told. Balance in a debate or interview. Balance in work and family, often the toughest of all.

I was working relentlessly with little time for reflection or the creative thought I thrive on. Calls in the middle of the night, weekends interrupted, vacations cancelled or curtailed had become a way of life. My children were growing up. Birthdays and holidays and milestones all ran together. It seemed dad was always on the phone or preoccupied with work. I love the journalism, but I had lost my balance. Balance and integrity go hand-in-hand.

So I decided to build a new platform for myself. I would teach and make documentaries. I would engage issues in a different and deeper way. I would pursue my definition of success. I would redefine the challenge and restore the balance. The move would constitute a dramatic and difficult turning point, but it was driven by my firm belief that change and challenge, built upon principle and considered purpose, are also elements of a rewarding life.

But a difficult decision became excruciating. I announced my departure on September 10, 2001 – one day before the terror attacks on The World Trade Center and Pentagon. In that instant, journalism assumed an urgent, new mission. Or perhaps it was merely reminded that there was a higher purpose than the non-stop talk of scandal and missing interns. Suddenly, there was an important, historic story to tell.

I decided to extend my time at CNN for a while longer. In the aftermath of 9/11, the Washington bureau needed leadership, and I wanted to contribute to the early reporting of this most remarkable story. Even as we tried to do our jobs, we also had to deal with the anthrax scare and our own security procedures. I wanted to be sure the bureau was safe and the coverage properly launched.

But I would keep my plans on track. My priorities had not changed. Nor had the basic issues confronting daily journalism. In many ways, the moment starkly exposed a void in our national discourse and presented an opportunity. Beyond the fire drill of moment-by-moment news coverage, there was a place for storytelling whose purpose was to inform, engage, and teach us something bigger and broader about our world. 9/11 made the challenge even more poignant. My objective – to get some balance and challenge myself with the discipline of deeper study – was as relevant as ever.

Finally, a most personal consideration. When I married my wife, I made a commitment to be a full partner in our family, to work really hard, and to contribute and to build. Integrity is about keeping your word. And the most important word or vow I ever made was to my wife. Integrity starts at home.

Frank Sesno serves as Professor of Public Policy and Communication at George Mason University, Virginia while working on a variety of documentary projects.

JOHN **B**ALDWIN is a general and vascular surgeon. Before going to Vietnam, he specialized in open-heart surgery but decided upon the broader fields of general and vascular surgery, he says, "to give my people skills more room to flourish." For his service as Chief of Thoracic Surgery with the 24th Evacuation Hospital, Baldwin received the Bronze Star. His story makes clear why his integrity is so vitally important.

As a surgeon trained as a scientist and a healer, I learned early in my career that absolute integrity is essential for success. Absolute integrity – the ability to honor and recognize the truth and follow through with appropriate action at work, at home, in marriage, with your children, and with yourself. This is the ingredient of great men and women and shines out of their eyes like a lamp in the night. This has been my goal and my obligation to those who have entrusted and allowed me to operate and handle their very beings, their stilled hearts, and their living, breathing organs.

Baldwin's story of inspiration happened Thanksgiving Day, 1968, while he was a major in the United States Army serving in Vietnam.

I had been at the 24th Evacuation Hospital near Bien Hoa, since May, and was chief of chest and vascular surgery, and after the first two weeks of disbelief and homesickness had settled into the routine of over one thousand casualties a month, an average of twelve major operations a day and constant outgoing artillery. I had seen it all: rocket wounds, Claymore mine injuries, gunshot wounds, *punji* stick gangrene, and napalm burns. We thought we were pretty good, and we were. Our place prided itself in saying, "If

What Do You Stand For?

you get to the 24th, we will get you home."

The radio crackled in the surgical *Quonset*. A chopper was bringing in four American wounded. None of the wounded, all GI's, made a sound. Four teams of nurses, doctors and corpsmen went to work, cutting off clothes, drawing blood, starting IV's and assessing priorities.

I was summoned almost immediately to attend to the most urgent of those casualties, a young man, aged 21, named Bruce Clark, an E-4, who had been in-country for just a week. While training with live hand-grenades from a pit trench with several of his company, a soldier, two down from him, had dropped a grenade in the pit, and everyone froze. They were too green to know they had four seconds to pick it up and throw it, and too frightened to move. The resulting explosion killed four and severely wounded Clark. My initial rapid assessment was difficult because he was covered with mud, torn uniform, and blood, but it was obvious he needed a quick trip to the O.R. if he were to live.

Four hours later, with the combined talents of the "A Team" anesthesiologist, ophthalmologist, orthopedist, neuro-surgeon, and myself, Bruce Clark entered the recovery room. Swathed in bandages from head to his knees, this once-handsome high school athlete from Cumberland, Rhode Island had been "saved," but reduced to one arm, no legs, no eyes, a profusion of tubes and wires going in and out, and painful incisions in his abdomen and left chest. Our angels of mercy, the army nurse corps, surrounded him with love and care.

In the mess hall, turkey with all the trimmings was laid out in grand style, but I was too tired to eat. I went back and made rounds on the dozen or so kids that I had operated upon over those last twenty-four hours, and made a special stop to see Bruce Clark. I was the one who had to tell him that he would never see again, and that walking would be very, very difficult. He never asked me, "then why did you let me live?"

In the weeks that followed, Bruce Clark required several more operations, and incredible amounts of daily care to survive. He endured pain most men could never understand, all in the inky blackness of his sightlessness. We became quite close; indeed, he became bonded to me and dependent upon me. I became his big brother and his dad. I was there when the general pinned the Purple Heart on his pillow, and when it was finally safe for him to make the 3,000 mile journey to the 249th Field Hospital in Tokyo, my commander allowed me to accompany him. I was his contact with reality on the big C-141 Starlifter as it winged its way across the South China Sea, carrying Bruce and one hundred other American wounded farther and farther from the killing fields.

I bade him a tearful farewell on January 5, 1969, in a clean, sunny, well-appointed ward with the finest American nurses and doctors that ever were. He, the soldier, just a kid; I now thirty-five, the surgeon, his companion on the road to recovery. "I can't cry, Major Baldwin," he said. "My tear makers must have been taken out with my eyes." "I know," I said, unashamedly weeping as I hugged him goodbye, knowing that we would never meet again in this world.

I returned to Vietnam, finished my tour, and came home to a strange country that did not understand where I had been or what we had done; much less why we were still doing it. My family and I visited the Vietnam Memorial Wall in Washington, D.C., in 1986. I was shocked to find his name, on panel 34W, line 47. "Ground casualty, died, accidental self-destruction, January 21, 1969," said the inscription in the book-like directory. (This referred to the dropped hand grenade, but could not convey the suffering that followed and the unexpected death after reaching safety in Japan.) I ran my fingers across his name engraved in the cold black marble...BRUCE A. CLARK. What had happened? An infection I had missed? A blood clot to the lungs? Some hidden fragment that became a catastrophe? Again the tears came, this time enough for both of us. I turned to hold my wife and said, "Maybe that was the best way for him. I just don't know."

Bruce was only one of many. A young man who never got to own a car, go to college, propose marriage, have children, take kids to a Sunday doubleheader at Fenway Park or any of the thousands of things we all take for granted. Devastated by the loss of their son, the Clarks moved from Cumberland shortly thereafter and I have never been able to find them to tell them of the bravery of their son and how I loved him.

And then there is now. Bruce and the nearly two thousand American soldiers that I had the privilege to operate upon remain indelibly written on my heart. Somewhere between that emotional day of farewell on the ward in Tokyo and several years later, it became apparent to me that my life must stand for something more than the ordinary, if the sacrifice of the Bruce Clarks was to have real meaning. It was their example of courage, bravery and unquestioning devotion, which inspired me to become the person that I am now.

In honor of their memory, I have tried to elevate my standards of absolute integrity to meet their expectations. I treasure life, children, honesty, valor, duty, country, and family; all things that Bruce and the 57,000 other names on the Wall never got to practice or experience. I cannot dishonor their sacrifice by living my own life in a manner unworthy of their suffering.

This poem by W.H. Auden, which is inscribed by the grave of the Gallant Warrior (Great Britain's Unknown) in Westminster Abbey, says it best:

"*To save your world, you asked this man to die,*
Would this man, could he see you now, ask 'Why?'"

6

a powerful antidote

THE ETHICAL VALUE OF RESPECT goes beyond being courteous and polite. "The dignity of *all* people," Michael Josephson of the Josephson Institute of Ethics says, "is the core tenet of respect. An important way of treating others with respect is to tolerate other people's beliefs and accept individual differences without prejudice."

Intolerance – political, cultural, and religious – is the greatest issue facing us today. Intolerance excludes us from the world. It takes us away from our connection to humanity and leads us down a path to fear, hate and conflict.

Tolerance opens our minds and hearts to others. Acceptance leads us to greater understanding and peace.

"Tolerance," President John Kennedy once said, "implies no lack of commitment to one's own beliefs. Rather it condemns the oppression or persecution of others."

STANLEY CROUCH is a jazz critic, author and essayist. His work has been described as acerbic, combative, incisive and eloquent. His column in the *New York Daily News* speaks with clarity and common sense. Crouch's radar is sensitive to hypocrisy and pretense, but he makes it clear that "Human frailty, greed, and ruthlessness are freely distributed through the gene pool. We need to be neither cynical nor naïve, just mature enough to face the facts and keep going forward."

I think the most important thing is to truly try to deal with people as individuals and recognize that each case is an individual case. After all is said and done, each person is one person.

In the '60s, when I was a kid, I bought into – very uncomfortably – that whole kind of Black Nationalist conception where we just lumped all white people together, like this cold-hearted Frosty-the-Snowman type, you know? That's why I fight so hard against it now because I know it not only distorts what the world is like, but it does something very bad to you internally. It causes you to impose limited human identification of oneself.

The reality is society's becoming more and more integrated, regardless of what anyone says. You see more and more young people across race, hanging out, laughing with each other, wearing the same outrageously tasteless clothing, the same hideous music, going to buy the same vile fast foods, talking to each other about their common experiences with MTV, VH-1, various television shows that they've been looking at since they were children and on it goes.

American civilization points toward deeper and richer integration, and nobody can stop it. It just goes back to that thing that is oft' quoted and needs to be quoted forever – someday, you know, there'll be an America in which all of our children, not just the black ones, but all of our children, will be judged by the content of their character not the color of their skin, not their religion, not their class, not anything that could be used to obviate their individual humanity. And I think that's where we're going. That's what I'm fighting for. My whole battle is with that.

KEN BURNS has been a filmmaker for twenty years with biographical documentaries covering Thomas Jefferson, Frank Lloyd Wright, and Lewis and Clark. But it is on the canvas of life-size events that Burns shines the brightest, where he shows us who we are as a country and a people. He highlights our successes and our failures with equal light because he knows that both aspects reveal our national character.

Baseball remains my personal favorite. Through the history of our "national pastime" are played-out classic struggles, showing us our virtues, and our vices, but perhaps more importantly, how we keep trying to get it right, perfect the play, improve the score, and get better as we go.

The most powerful guiding principle in my life has been and is now the conviction that the past is indeed *prologue* and we cannot know where we are headed if we do not understand from whence we came. From this, we can clearly see the futility of racism, for instance, which is the end result of the need to point the finger, blame, and vilify our neighbor in order to escape personal responsibility for our own perceived miseries.

Soon after *The Civil War* [the documentary] came out, I was giving a big speech in Wilmington, Delaware, and a young girl – maybe twelve or thirteen years old – asked me a question. "What is racism?" And I looked at her and I realized how important a question it was for her to ask and to understand. And I said that it was probably the horrible, terrible, flip side of a very understandable human emotion, which is love of one's own. And when that love of one's own metastasizes into hate, we begin to make distinctions about other people based on their differences from us. And what could be a more obvious, and yet superficial, difference than the color of one's skin.

The first of many "moments of principle," or moments of consciousness, is the moment when Jackie Robinson stepped into the previously all-white baseball world of the Dodgers and changed everything.

I think that we, in the media culture, confuse heroism. We have reduced the notion that anybody who is well known, a celebrity, is therefore some sort of hero. In the area of sports, anybody who plays their game well is also a hero. And I would like to vehemently disagree. I think that heroes are very interesting combinations of both strengths and weaknesses. A hero is not someone who is perfect. Indeed, what the Greeks have told us for thousands of years, that the nature of a hero is the very obvious strengths and weaknesses of the people and the negotiations that go on between them which renders our contemporary scene with far more heroes than our media would like us to believe.

Jackie Robinson is a particularly great hero because he transcended the skill that it takes to be a Major League ballplayer and entered the realm of almost Biblical proportions when he exhibited the necessary forbearance to withstand the withering racism that took place as the first African-American to join Major League Baseball.

We had called it "our national pastime." But, how could it be a national pastime when many of the best players – as it turns out, some of the greatest players ever – were, for decades under a gentleman's agreement, excluded from playing this game and were forced to develop separate but athletically equal leagues. But it all goes back to the ability of the experiment of Robinson to be a success. That it was based on the nature of his character, his principles, his willingness to turn the other cheek, to exhibit that kind of Biblical forbearance, that turns it into one of the great dramas – not just in American history, not just in sports history, but in all of human history.

I've always been drawn, emotionally and psychologically, to the fault line that has bedeviled and, I think, ennobled our country's experiment since its inception, and that is the fault line of race. When Thomas Jefferson wrote our creed, "All men are created equal," he owned more than two hundred human beings and never saw fit, in his lifetime, to free them. And, so, he set in motion the kind of hypocrisy that would take a civil war to eliminate, and the frustration of waiting so many decades for Jackie Robinson to emerge.

My mother had cancer all of my life and died when I was eleven years old. This occurred almost simultaneously with the great progress of civil rights in the early 1960s. I remember that I would be paralyzed as a child staying up all night with great anxiety after I had seen the fire hoses and the dogs turned on the protesters in Selma, or learned of the murder of four black girls in a church, or the disappearance of three civil rights workers. All of these things plagued me in proportions just inconceivable for someone who is eight, nine, ten, and eleven years old. And I realized much later that I had redirected the anxieties I had over the cancer that was killing my family to the cancer that was killing my country.

Dr. King always says it best – that I, Ken Burns, look forward to that moment when we rise up and live out the true meaning of our creed. And what's great about this country is the other end of that mysterious sentence – of Jefferson's hypocrisy about "All men are created equal," in which he says, "Life, liberty and the pursuit of *happiness.*" Now, he could've said, "Life, liberty and the pursuit of *property,*" like the philosopher John Locke, who was his intellectual mentor and we would have lived in a far different country; but he said "the pursuit of happiness." And the key word there is *pursuit.*

Most countries see themselves as an end in and of themselves. We Americans see ourselves as improvable, always improving, and I like that about the country. So the mystery of that wonderful statement, "pursuit of happiness," I think is what's animated our desire always to get better. And that's going to be in racial dimensions, it's going to be in personal dimensions, it's going to be in almost every field of human endeavor I can imagine. I like being part of a country that's in the process of becoming.

THERE'S BEEN A LOT OF DEBATE in the last several years about the nature of a hero. This was one of many things that changed after September 11th. I explored this issue with another contributor, former Marine Captain Dale Dye. He reveals that critical situations transform some individuals to act out of a larger purpose – a basic respect for their fellow man.

I would say a hero has two basic qualities: a selfless devotion to what's right, whether that's his duty or not, and the courage of his convictions. That's simplistic but the classic example, of course, is the firemen and policemen who went into the World Trade Center and the Pentagon. Look, that was a dangerous situation. Everybody knew it was a dangerous situation. But those folks had a higher devotion of doing something larger than themselves. It wasn't just about a job at that point. Nobody is going to die for a job. They were outside themselves.

We have a long history as human beings, regardless of nationality, of basing our ethos on specific heroes; people, who demonstrated a larger view of things, who think, feel, and respond outside themselves. And *thinking* is sometimes a confusing term. I don't think genuine heroes spend a lot of time contemplating that issue. I think they instinctively feel it as – this is right. And if you were to press them, in many cases, they probably couldn't tell you why other than some vague notion. And that's okay. It's not necessary that our heroes be massive intellectuals. It's only important that they do what needs doing in critical situations.

But let's take it out of a catastrophic event or combat situation. Let's say you have a really good friend who's involved in something that's untoward. You can say to yourself, "Look, no skin off my nose. That's what he wants to do. He's a big boy and can do whatever he wants, and I'll be here if he needs me." Well, that's not courageous. What's courageous is you say, I'm more concerned about him than I am about me, so I'll confront him. I'll say, "Listen, you know this isn't right. You know this is something that you shouldn't be doing. Why are you doing it? If there's a way I can help you, I will help you."

You may have known this guy for thirty-five, forty years. May be your best pal. And he says, "Well, screw you. You're not my buddy. If you're going to poke your nose inside my life, if you're going to impose your morality on me, then you're not a friend. You're just some right-thinking wacko." And that's very hurtful, but you stand your ground. You may lose the guy that you've loved for thirty-five years. And yet you have the courage of your convictions.

On June 28, 2000, the United States Supreme Court held that the Boy Scouts of America could exclude homosexual boys and leaders from their organization.

On October 17, the County Board of Supervisors in Santa Barbara, California met to consider two resolutions put forth by the County Administrator and the Human Relations Commission that the Board vote to "end any and all financial or in-kind support of the Boy Scouts of America," based on what the HRC believed to be discriminatory practices.

Speaking on behalf of the local Los Padres Council of the Boy Scouts was Executive Director Len Lanzi.

I am an Eagle Scout. I've been in Scouting for 30 years, since I was eight years old. I have been working for the Boy Scouts for fourteen years, most recently in the capacity of Executive Director here for the past three-and-a-half years. I'm in a very unique position today to speak as the official spokesperson of the Boy Scouts of America; also to speak as a County resident and a person who feels very deeply about the issue at hand.

I want to remind the Supervisors of one thing – this really isn't about the Boy Scouts. It's about a bunch of kids. It's about the values that parents choose for their children to learn and to articulate and to grow up in. When I joined 30 years ago, my parents wanted me...to learn how to be trustworthy, loyal, helpful, friendly, courteous, kind, obedient, cheerful, thrifty, brave, clean, and reverent. They wanted me to learn how to help other people at all times, to be a good citizen, to be morally straight, physically fit.

We are a private organization. We do have membership standards for some of our programs. There are people both inside and outside the Boy Scouts who disagree with

our membership standards. But they are our standards…
We welcome all people to be in our organization as long as
they have our beliefs. If they don't have our beliefs, they
don't have to join. That's the simple message that we're giving to people.

We don't hate gay people. We teach our boys to be courteous, to be friendly, and to be kind. We teach them to help
other people at all times. We don't say that homosexuals are
child abusers, because they're not. They're not pedophiles.
And [homophobic people] put those arguments…in the Boy
Scouts' mouths. But I'm here to tell you officially that that is
not true. They [Boy Scouts of America] say that an avowed
homosexual is someone that we don't want in our organization. I'm not quite sure what that means.

…I'm here to urge the Board not to support either one
of the resolutions that have been put forward by the
Human Relations Commission. I think they're mean-spirited.
I think they're made to make a statement about the Boy
Scouts that is detrimental to kids. And that's what we're
here about. We're here about kids.

In recent weeks, the Boy Scouts has been in the spot-
light due to the United States Supreme Court ruling…Peo-
ple in the community have tried to make it a point to turn
this into a very personal vendetta against the Boy Scouts
and against me, in particular.

I know there are many people in this room that
understand that I am a private person who keeps my personal relationships private. But I am gay. And I uphold the
Boy Scouts policies because I believe in them. …I would

not have worked for the Boy Scouts if I didn't agree that we save kid's lives, that we do not hurt people, that *my* job is to make sure every boy in this county has the opportunity to join because the *value* that we give kids is incredible.

...I also feel very strongly about what Pacific Pride and the gay advocacy groups here in town do because I think people are discriminated against, and we have to eradicate that from the public part of our world. But we have to agree that there are private organizations that serve different constituencies and we can't serve everybody together....

I've made my statement today because I feel very strongly that, as a Scout, I have to have integrity. I have to be credible. And I know that there are people in this room that have information about me personally, and I couldn't not speak up without feeling hypocritical. I'm trustworthy. I'm loyal. I'm helpful, friendly, courteous, kind, obedient, cheerful, thrifty, brave, clean, and reverent.

After watching Lanzi's statement on the local news that night, I was struck by two things. Here was a man who sincerely believed in the principles of scouting, had achieved the level of Eagle Scout, reached the office of Scout Executive, and was well on his way to a career and example of the highest qualities that we think of, when we think of a Boy Scout. At the same time, he felt the need to stand up and be accountable to those very qualities even at the risk of great personal loss.

If we define ethics as Michael Josephson says, "as having the character and the courage to do the right thing even when it costs more than you want to pay," then here is a man who clearly demonstrates that. Not only was he standing by an organization whose policy of exclusion personally stood against him, but he was putting forth a passionate argument to local elected officials not to cut off any support for the local organization.

This story shows what happens when judgments are degraded by prejudice and discrimination. It shows how others rise above that prejudice to take an unpopular stand. Ultimately, it's about how each of us can best demonstrate the principle of respect by being open to other people who may be different from ourselves and not treat people harshly just because they are different.

The day after Lanzi spoke to county supervisors, October 18th, he was asked to resign his position. When he refused, he was suspended with pay.

I contacted Len Lanzi to learn more about the events that led up to his "moment of principle," but due to a confidentiality clause in a legal settlement with the Boy Scouts, he could not talk about the Boy Scouts, their policies, or the events that led up to his statement.

Soon after, news reports appeared about his abrupt termination and the resignation of two board members, Dennis Peterson and Karl Eberhard, from the Los Padres Council. Because of their own stands and to learn more about the events surrounding this issue, I contacted them.

DENNIS PETERSON moved to Santa Barbara in the late sixties. Looking for greater community involvement, a friend suggested the local chapter of the Boy Scouts.

Peterson describes himself as "a former Marine combat command officer in Vietnam who is a fiscal conservative and a social moderate still with a streak of duty to do the right thing."

Peterson was out-of-town when he heard Len Lanzi's statement before the county Supervisors while watching the news.

Although Lanzi's purpose before County Supervisors was to appeal for continued financial support of the local organization in light of the Supreme Court ruling, the focus remained on his simple, declarative statement, "I am gay."

"Personally, it was never an issue for me," Peterson said. "Not to say that I wondered about it. I know that other [Board] members, perhaps, had thought about it and decided, well, what difference does it make? He's doing a fine job. What do we care? But then the president of the Board suspended him. I know [the president] real well. He's a nice guy, but I don't think [he] really understands the gay issue. [He] said to Len, 'Well, you can *change*, can't you?'"

When Peterson returned home, he was contacted by the Council president. "'According to Scout national policy,' he said, 'I've suspended Len as Council Executive. I hope you'll support me.' And I said, I just can't do it."

About an hour later, Peterson drafted a letter of resignation and hand-delivered it. *"As a Board member, I'm upset with your unilateral decision to suspend Len without Board action...My own personal views and the 'official' BSA view are at odds...It's not hard to remember 30 years ago and our country's struggle over Civil Rights. Have we now replaced 'black' with 'homosexual'?"*

This is about human dignity. I remember talking to my wife when I got home and realized I couldn't be a part of this. This is a sham! How can we teach young men the things we try to teach them – about character and respect – and at the same time do this to another human being? It's just *wrong!*

I have a son who's an Eagle Scout. He was outraged, absolutely outraged when he heard what happened to Len. He still has his Eagle badge, though. We encouraged him to keep it. I think he sees it more as a case of his own individual achievement.

A lot of the anti-gay movement is based on the fact that if we have gay men around our young men, they're going to *corrupt* them, put their hands on them. And yet, according to the statistics that I'm aware of, most pedophiles are heterosexual men. We had a classic case out of Santa Maria about ten years ago where a Mormon, a heterosexual male, married, kids, Boy Scout leader, was "fooling" with his boys. A Mormon lawyer, of all things! They busted him and allegedly, he was sent back to Salt Lake to undergo some counseling, was certified by Salt Lake as being squared away and back on the straight and narrow – and he did it again!

What is troubling to me is that the Boy Scouts of America is the only scouting organization in the whole world that has this issue. It's not Scouts of Canada. It's not Scouts of England, or Scouts of Mexico, or anywhere else. Just the Boy Scouts of America, in a country that is supposed to stand for a higher form of tolerance than we're showing here.

It's education. I think about my own transformation from the time I was a Lieutenant in the Marine Corps – gays were the worst thing *ever!* My roommate in Basics school was gay. He was a fine Marine, a fine man, and a great guy.

Look, these are human rights issues. It's not about alleged "lifestyle" choices. We are what we are, and we have to deal with people as we take them, and it's nobody's business to go around and change them.

KARL EBERHARD is an architect in Santa Barbara and was a Board member since 1992. After learning of Lanzi's suspension, he voiced his opinion at the Council's General Board Meeting on November 14, 2000, and then walked out. "It was a stirring speech, but I don't think it changed anyone's mind."

After the Council president placed Len on leave, the Board contemplated what they should do. At this point, the national office sent out a nicely packaged "help deal." They sent out a temporary Scout Executive. They sent out legal advice. They covered all the salaries and made it very convenient. And then national withdrew his [Lanzi's] commission, which is a necessary requirement to be a Scout Executive.

At the Board meeting, there were clearly three camps. A third of the people actually thought that this was the right thing to do. You know, gay people are a bad influence on young people and somehow it's a disease and if children hang out with gay people they might catch it. Another third of the people were scared because national made it *very* clear that if we didn't behave *exactly* the way they told us to, they'd yank the charter of the Council. The final third were on the fence. So two-thirds of the people were inclined to fire him. But they didn't fire him because he's gay. They fired him because national had decommissioned him!

I grew up with Scouting. My father made canoes for my scout troop. It's been part of my life. So, I joined the local group to promote Scouting and youth activities that are healthy and teaches them to be good people. I mean they're a good group, but they're a group with a cancer. That's the bottom line. I have small children, but if my son comes to me wanting to join the Scouts, I'm going to tell him, no. I wouldn't give him the choice to join the Ku Klux Klan, either! I don't want him joining any organization that discriminates. I want him to meet all types of people. I want him to know people who are of different religions and have different sexual orientations so that he understands the world around him properly. Scouting is not doing that.

I think the Boy Scouts has every right to discriminate. I fully agree with that. I don't think they should be getting any public money or public assistance, of any kind, if they are going to discriminate. But it's their *right* to discriminate. Just like the Ku Klux Klan has the right to exist. I disagree *completely* with them on every subject, but they have a right to exist.

Promoting tolerance, that's a hard one. I think the best we can do is to be a positive example in respecting all people. I guess that's why I resigned the Board in a rather vocal and public forum. I wanted to make a point of the fact that somebody needs to stand up and say this is wrong.

There is a Board member, however, who disagreed with the decision and chose to *remain* on the Board – an attorney by the name of Alan Courtney.

ON THE EVENING OF NOVEMBER 2, a Confidential Executive Board Meeting of the local Los Padres Council was held to specifically address Lanzi's future as Scout Executive as well as the position of Boy Scouts of America's national headquarters. In attendance were 36 members of the Executive Board, along with the Board president, the Regional Director from Los Angeles, the national organization's legal counsel, as well as an attorney who argued national's case before the U.S. Supreme Court.

Alan Courtney attended all meetings involving Len Lanzi's case. His perspective comes from discussions with many of those involved as well as his agenda notes from those meetings. His decision to *remain* on the Council's Board is remarkable not only because he opposed the action and the means by which it took place, but his family has been and continues to be close friends with Lanzi.

> When I attended the Confidential Executive Board Meeting, I was surprised to discover that the General Counsel for the Boy Scouts of America was there. He had flown in from Texas, along with an attorney who had successfully argued the case (BSA v. Dale) in front of the Supreme Court. This seemed very unusual to me.
>
> The General Counsel made it clear that national would take care of all of the attorneys' fees and pay any damages. Whatever happened out of this, essentially,

national was taking it away from us at the local level.

Prior to the meeting, I had gotten a copy of the rules the Boy Scouts have regarding their professional staff. They are given a commission, and there are references to [giving an employee] notice and a hearing and a right to confront witnesses. Now, this group was saying that they were going to 'pull' his commission. And so I asked the attorney, there are all these procedures here that you're supposed to follow before you can pull someone's commission. Why aren't you following these procedures with Len? And one attorney said, "Well, it's like he's an ax murderer." Those were her exact words. "It's like he's an admitted ax murderer. There's absolutely no defense to this, so there's really no need to go through with all those procedures." And I thought where did she learn this?

What was shocking was that everybody sat there nodding their heads. I brought up the argument that the Scouts and the Nazis now had something in common, both persecuting gays.

"There's absolutely no way you can make that analogy," they said. "This has absolutely nothing to do with National Socialism. This is about values." They kept going back to this whole thing on values, and that they believe that it is a *conscious* decision on the part of a man or a woman to become gay. And I said I didn't wake up one morning and decide I liked girls. Well, gee, I don't know if I like boys or girls. Let me think about it and I'll make a decision.

After that confidential meeting another General meeting of the Board was scheduled to decide whether to terminate

What Do You Stand For?

Len as the Council Executive. Before that meeting I called a meeting for all the people in my district. The vast majority of the people who were there all said to vote *against* firing Len. It was like 19 to 1.

So, I went to the [November 14] General Board meeting. Part of the argument was, if we keep Len, how do we handle a potential loss of financial support from some people who traditionally supported Scouting? However, if we terminate him, we're going to lose financial support. No matter which decision you make, you were going to lose some, financially. There was also discussion concerning the fact that we were going to drive away a lot of members. The other argument was that we would lose membership if we *keep* him as head of the Council. It kind of went round and round.

I got into it with one of the members because he was saying that this is about values; that this whole thing is about standing up for values. And I said, it's not values. It's bigotry. And I'm not a bigot. I've never been a bigot. And I'm not going to be a bigot.

Before the vote, there was a very impassioned argument by one of the members. This gentleman asked [the Regional Director], "What exactly is the reason for this policy? Why don't we allow gay men or women to serve as leaders or as employees?

[The Director] said, "Because they don't provide good role models to young boys."

Then the gentleman said, "It's my understanding that, 10 to 20% of the population is gay. That means that we have gay, teenage boys. Don't we have a responsibility to provide *them* with good role models?"

"No. No. No! [the Director said.] They shouldn't even be members!"

The vote was to terminate Len.

At that point, Karl Eberhard got up and said, "I'm out of here and I quit." I was very tempted to do the same.

I got a call the next day from the President of the Council because I wasn't supporting the policy. He asked me to resign. I told him that I represent my district and that they elected me to the board. And when they don't want me on the board anymore, I'll leave. But I don't serve at his pleasure. He asked me what my religion was, and I said that it really is none of his business and that I'd never, ever, in Scouting, been asked that question. Then he started quoting from the Old Testament about how this is a mortal sin in the eyes of God. And I said, but Scouting is not a religious movement. It's open to all religions. So if you're basing this on a Christian interpretation of the Bible, then what are we becoming now? Fundamentalist Christians were having their way.

I said that since this issue had come up, that I didn't feel comfortable putting on a Scout uniform anymore. I was driving to a meeting and I got out at a gas station in my uniform. And I was looking over my shoulder because it was just so uncomfortable. And he says, well, he didn't have that problem because he didn't have a uniform. I'm thinking, you're the president of the Council and you don't have a Scout uniform!

I told him that I wasn't leaving, that it was my intention to stay on and try to work for change within the organization. I didn't want the organization being hijacked by any group.

So, I took the decision back to my district. And because nobody in my district is in support of excluding gays, what we decided to do, as a district, was to go along with a path of what we call "passive non-cooperation." We're not raising money for the Council. We're not supporting the Council in any of its activities. All we're doing is focusing on the program for the boys as far as camping and hiking, things like that.

I agree with the Supreme Court's decision. I agree that the government cannot tell a private organization who to admit or not admit as members. But I've read that decision and at the very beginning the Supreme Court says they are not passing on the *wisdom* of the decision. And I think the Boy Scouts have made a very *unwise* decision.

I think there are two different Scouting programs. There's the camping, hiking, compass and maps – things you think about with Scouting, which is the reality. And I think the *illusion* is that there's all this strong morality and religious training and that we're using this program for that reason so that people will donate money to the Scouts. But you don't see it with the boys.

All I can hope for is just slow, incremental changes. I have to look over all adult volunteers in this Council and my district. I don't ask them about their sexual orientation. I don't ask them about their religion. We are not going out and recruiting gay leaders or openly opposing it. We're not enforcing national's policy of a ban on gays. We're essentially ignoring it. I don't know if that's really the wise thing to do here because there are times when I just want to quit. The reason I stay is the program. It's the tradition. It's the very reason why this was set up in the first place by Lord Baden-Powell, the founder of Scouting. He was a hero in the Boer War in South Africa. He discovered that a lot of soldiers were dying unnecessarily because they couldn't figure out how to get water or what to eat or how to build a fire. Scouting was originally set up to teach outdoor skills to boys and to teach them things that would save their lives.

My oldest son now is in the Marine Corps, and it looks like he's going to Afghanistan. And I'm very happy that he's had all the training that I could give him while he was in Scouts. Maybe that will save his life.

Since leaving the Los Padres Board, Dennis Peterson and his wife serve as volunteers for both the Tres Condados Girls Scouts Council and Habitat for Humanity. Karl Eberhard is continuing his community involvement by serving in the Rotary Club and as a board member on the Community Housing Association, a non-profit group committed to developing low-income housing.

In January 2002, Alan Courtney received the Los Padres Council of Boy Scouts Silver Beaver award – the highest honor a volunteer can receive at the Council level – for "distinguished service to youth." In accepting the award, Courtney told the audience, "I'm dedicating it to my good friend Len Lanzi." Then, Courtney said, "All the air left the room."

Len Lanzi currently works as Director of Development for Junior Achievement of Southern California. In addition, he is a member of the Tres Condados Girls Scouts Council Advisory Board, and the Log Cabin Republican Club in Los Angeles.

On page fifty of the current (11th edition) of the Boy Scout Handbook, kindness is defined: *"We live in a world that has more than its share of anger, fear, and war. Extending kindness to those around you and having compassion for all people is a powerful antidote to the poisons of hatred and violence."*

7

do justly

WHAT IS JUSTICE? What is a just individual?

These two questions have been the focus of philosophical debate probably since the first man expressed himself in argument with another. Plato's immense dialogue, *The Republic,* is given over to a discussion about these very questions with no truly satisfying answers emerging.

Determining what is fair can sometimes be daunting. Whether it's considering an equal share of pie or equal opportunity, a variety of stakeholders, each with his or her own conflicting interests, rarely agree on what is fair.

At its core, fairness is about being open-minded and committed to the equitable treatment of all involved, a willingness to suspend prejudice and consider all relevant information. It also means voluntarily correcting a personal or organizational mistake or impropriety and not taking unfair advantage of the mistakes or ignorance of others.

Perhaps the most persuasive definition is best seen by example. Author H. Jackson Brown, Jr. said, "Live so that when your children think of fairness and integrity, they think of you."

FILM CRITIC AND CONTRIBUTOR LEONARD MALTIN described a 'moment of fairness.'

> I once wrote a book that took years to complete; it was a true labor of love. To my dismay, I received a snide, churlish review in a major newspaper from a person I hadn't met at the time, who (it turns out) was working on a book of his own about the same topic.
>
> Many years later, *The New York Times Book Review* asked me if I would be interested in reviewing that very book. The temptation was strong, but I couldn't succumb. I told the editor that I'd once received a bad review from this author, and didn't think I could give the book a fair hearing. She thanked me for my candor, and I shook my head at a lost opportunity.
>
> "Can I ask a favor," I added as we said good-bye. "Could you try to find someone else who wouldn't like it either?"

AS A POLICE OFFICER AND DETECTIVE, ROB ARCHEY has worked from the roughest inner-city district of Baltimore, Maryland to the blue-collar city of Altoona, Pennsylvania. We've all read stories about police officers involved in ethics-related scandals. In reality, the majority go about their jobs with a diligence to service and a sincere commitment to a clear-cut code of conduct.

I try to carry my personal values with me when I put on my badge. In reality, they can't be separated. There is hardly a day that passes without my praying for strength, wisdom and courage. That is something I do before I leave the police locker room.

I have made a conscious effort to be honest. I've found that even the most vile, dishonest criminal expects honesty of a police officer. Many become absolutely indignant and genuinely disappointed if they believe that a cop has not kept his word. I believe that deep inside – even in the most hardened criminal – there is a youngster who, at some time in his life, looked at the Lawman as a hero, whose honesty was always above reproach. This is true. I've seen it.

I was investigating a series of four robberies that I believe were committed by the same person. It took months of investigation, but I finally had enough evidence for a case against "Mike" – a 35-year-old heroin addict – for one of the robberies.

Once in custody, I interviewed Mike. As a result, he confessed to all four robberies. My training and experience has shown me that unless a person is a total sociopath, he wants to tell the truth to someone. Sometimes the burden of guilt is more troubling than the prospect of going to jail.

After his admission, Mike voiced concern about another robbery case in which we had arrested "Ike" months earlier. Ike had committed a string of eight armed robberies. He was definitely the robber, but he lied and fought us all the way. As a result, Ike ended up with only months in jail. Mike, on the other hand, was facing 20 years in a state prison with his confessions putting the final nail in his successful prosecution.

Mike's honesty put him at risk of 20 years in prison, while Ike's obstruction bore the fruit of less than a year in jail. Mike could not see the fairness. I told him that telling the truth was the best thing for him. As he turned to go into the lock-up, Mike looked at me with resignation in his eyes and said, "Detective Archey, was telling the truth really the best thing for me?" As he walked away, I found myself torn between my sense of justice and my sense of fairness and mercy.

I laid down a set of rules when I interviewed Mike. He ended up playing by those rules. I determined that I would honor his decision to tell the truth by trying to help him when the plea agreement was formed.

I received subtle pressure from some of my peers and the assistant DA to "hammer" the guy. After all, we had him dead to rights, especially with the confession that I had obtained from him. I was tempted to renege on the rules that I had set earlier with Mike. You see, getting a robber heavy prison time is an accomplishment, and I would have looked better in the eyes of my fellow officers. All I can say to you is that I decided to be true to my convictions. And all that meant was that I was honest with myself.

In a perfect system, both Mike and Ike would be cooling their heels in prison for 20 years. But, it's not a perfect world. Never having promised Mike anything, I spoke to the District Attorney and the victims in the robbery cases. I explained to them my belief that Mike should be punished

What Do You Stand For?

for his crimes, while still being rewarded for his honesty in some way. As a result, Mike will be doing 3 1/2 to 7 years in state prison.

Mike may never fully appreciate what I did for him, and it doesn't really matter. I stood for what I believed to be honest and fair.

I've locked up more people than I can remember. But, I've never lied to one of them. They may fight me on the street or in court, but they will respect me. I have that respect from my peers, lawyers, judges, and yes, even the people that I've arrested. I wouldn't trade that respect for all the gold in the world.

DR. ROBERT BALLARD grew up wanting to be Captain Nemo from Jules Verne's *20,000 Leagues Under the Sea*. He's definitely got Nemo's thirst for search and adventure. Best known for his discovery of the *Titanic* in 1985, Ballard has explored a variety of notable shipwrecks including the German battleship *Bismarck* and the American carrier, *Yorktown*. President of the Institute for Exploration in Mystic Connecticut, Ballard's the kind of regular-guy explorer you'd want to hang out with because of his youthful enthusiasm. For Ballard, being open-minded in search of the truth is vital. As this story shows, his unbiased approach can lead to unexpected and exciting payoffs.

As a scientist, I would have to say this: do not have a vested interest in the answer to a question you are seeking an answer to. If you are biased, prejudicial, then that will influence you and cause you not to be completely honest in your search. I think a scientist needs to have a fundamental desire to know the answer but *not* to try to have the answer shape his or her perceived notions. Then they're not serving science. I think of Joe Friday in *Dragnet*, "Just the facts, Ma'am."

I play hunches a lot. I try to guess what's out there and try to position myself to be out there. Multiple hypotheses are a part of science. You come up with different ways of explaining something. But with each of them you try to fire a silver bullet through and only the truth will win. Only the truth cannot be killed. You may have a suspicion that it may be one of these five multiple hypotheses, but you shouldn't be so predisposed that you'll be disappointed if it isn't the one you thought it was. You should be surprised. You ought to have a smile on your face when it happens, not a frown.

There is a tremendous degree of serendipity. Once we were looking for hot springs in the deep sea and found unique animal communities living around them. We went there with a model. We were after missing heat energy. What we didn't realize was what might be a by-product of that discovery. Yes, we found the missing heat. But it was sort of dwarfed by what we found the consequences of it to be: the corollary, the secondary effect, which was the triggering of a carbon-based life system independent of the sun. We'd never *thought* about that as a consequence, and, yet, it was a wonderful surprise.

We came looking for something and found something

far more important. It just brings a smile to your face.

Beverly Torok is the swim coach for New Jersey's Westfield High School. With the state championship on the line, Coach Torok shows us that sometimes fairness trumps playing by the rules.

COACH TOROK'S RULES

- It's not whether you win or lose, it's *how* you play the game.
- Sportsmanship and a sense of fair play will be maintained at all times, under any circumstance, and will never be sacrificed for *any* reason.
- Sometimes even when you "lose," you "win."

These ideals are things that I constantly teach all of the student athletes I have coached. Case in point: New Jersey State Swimming Championship, March 2000.

With our team ahead on the scoreboard, in this very tight championship swim meet, a rule infraction was noticed. The opposing swimmers were assigned to the incorrect lanes. The infraction was actually an innocent, clerical error by a student manager from the opposing team. Though a rule violation, there was virtually no advantage gained by such a rule infraction. Nonetheless, the infraction resulting from this mistake would have, for all intents and purposes, ended the meet half way through and caused our team to be "handed" the state championship title.

I fully believe and teach faithfully "rules are rules." However, to win a championship in this fashion would have taken away the opportunity for our team to *win and thus earn* that title. We wanted to win the meet in the water and not on the pool deck. My decision to not protest, and continue the meet, did, however, result in the loss of our state title. Final Score: Westfield 84, Cherry Hill East 86.

The sportsmanship of our team and the spirit of the contest were maintained, but the championship was lost by 2 points, in the water. What our team "lost" that day, pales in comparison to the life lessons learned and accolades "won" from such a display of integrity and fair play. So, sometimes you "win" even when you "lose."

BORN IN JOHANNESBURG, SOUTH AFRICA, FW DEKLERK followed his father into politics after practicing law. He held several ministerial offices before becoming Leader of the National Party. After becoming State President of South Africa in 1989, deKlerk set about dismantling apartheid – the system by which white South Africans had tried to entrench their right to ethnic self-determination in an overwhelmingly black continent. When he released Nelson Mandela from prison in 1990, he set in motion a chain of events, which would lead to the first fully democratic elections in South Africa's history, on April 27, 1994.

For their work in bringing about meaningful change in the rule of government, deKlerk and Mandela were jointly awarded the Nobel Peace Prize in 1993.

What Do You Stand For?

I was brought up as a member of the *Gereformeerde Kerk* (Reformed Church) of South Africa. My family and ancestors played a leading role in the church, which had an especially strong influence on the development of the principles by which I have tried to lead my life. Apart from the basic Christian norms, the Reformed Church attached special importance to the concept of justice – which was further reinforced by my study and practice of the law. It was this sense of justice and my realization that the policies to which my party had previously been committed – were creating a situation in South Africa that was manifestly unjust, that played a major role in my decision to introduce the reforms that I announced on 2 February 1990.

The 'moment of principle' which I would like to mention is the decision which my colleagues in the Government and I took to initiate the far-reaching reforms which included the release of Mr. Nelson Mandela, the unbanning of all political parties and movements, and a clear commitment to the holding of constitutional negotiations to establish a fully democratic system in South Africa. This decision was not only pragmatic, but also based on the principle that South Africans should settle their differences through peaceful negotiations and that we should create a constitutional system in which all South Africa's individuals and communities would be treated equally and justly.

Rami Shapiro is an award-winning poet and essayist whose liturgical poems are used in prayer services throughout North

America. Two of his books have directly inspired me with their relevance to every day good sense – *Wisdom of the Jewish Sages* and *Minyan, 10 Principles for Living Life with Integrity*. His response not only reflects a conscious consideration of his principles but the honest challenge in living up to those principles in the "ordinary moments" of our lives.

I found this assignment quite challenging. The reason being that I seem to live by different principles on different days. So I have done my best to seek out the core principles that consciously guide my life. I underscore 'consciously' since I am smart enough to know I do many things that violate the conscious principles I seek to follow.

As a Jew and a rabbi, I seek to conform my life to the fundamental challenge of Torah: Be Holy as I, God, am Holy (Leviticus 19:2). What does it mean to be holy? The prophet Micah is my guide in this: "What does God require? Do justly, love mercy, and walk humbly with your God," (Micah 6:8). From this I understand holiness to be a commitment to justice, kindness, and spiritual intimacy.

So, if someone were to ask me, "What do you stand for – what principles guide your life," I would say this: I stand for being humanly holy, that is, for being just and kind in my dealings with women, men, and nature, and seeking a simple unity with God through prayer, meditation, and attending to the moment.

I find myself tested every day. Justice and kindness seem so clear until I try to live them in the ordinary moments of my everyday life. For example, just this morning a woman called, distraught about the betrayal of a friend. She wanted me to comfort her, to reinforce her sense of victimization. Yet as I listened to her story, I sensed very strongly that she was not innocent at all, that she had set the other up to betray her. Where is the justice in my vilifying her friend? Where is the kindness in ignoring her role in the matter? Yet, where is the holiness in making her feel worse?

This example may seem mundane. It is. I am not troubled by big tests of my principles. In those situations where my principles are being openly challenged and violated, I have a history of standing up for what I think is right. And I have yet to be confronted by a life and death challenge that would put me to the ultimate test. So it is the small things that gnaw at me: How to be kind to the driver who cut me off in traffic? How to be just when the little boys fighting in my school insist that the other is to blame? How to be holy in how I treat the things in my life: my car, my toothbrush, my shoes? How to be holy in how I earn and spend my money; how to be holy in how I speak to those I love and those I hate? Holiness is not a matter of martyrdom before the false gods of power. It is a matter of standing up to the constant pricks and briars of ordinariness.

So what did I say to the woman this morning? I won't say. If I tell you, it makes it sound easy. It isn't. Given my principles what would you say?

8

accountability

WALKING THE STREETS OF CHICAGO late one night, I found myself drawn to a magnificent gothic cathedral. Its intricate design and gargoyles stand as watchful security – more intimidating than any high-tech security system. On the front of the building were these words:

> "Give me Liberty to know, to utter and to argue freely according to my conscience, above all other liberties."
> –MILTON

Founded in 1847, the *Chicago Tribune* was established as a cathedral to free speech – to the public's right to know. Moving into the churchlike vestibule, I was immediately surrounded by more than two-dozen inscriptions carved into the travertine marble – all reflecting the values and responsibilities of a free press. Among the most compelling are those by Robert McCormick, one of the *Trib's* earliest and most prominent editor-publishers. They are words that both inspire and define journalism:

"The newspaper is an institution developed by modern civilization to present the news of the day, to foster commerce and industry, to inform and lead public opinion, and to furnish that check upon government which no constitution has ever been able to provide."

That "check" is at the heart of the ethical value of responsibility. Being responsible incorporates the values of accountability, self-restraint, and pursuit of excellence. A responsible person thinks about the consequences of his or her actions, is dependable, exercises self-control and sets a positive example.

Considering the ethical failures in the last several years, and the resulting crisis in confidence, the need for accountability has never been greater.

In the fall of 1982, Johnson & Johnson Chairman James Burke was confronted with a nightmare scenario. Seven people in the Chicago area had died after ingesting Extra-Strength Tylenol capsules that were laced with cyanide. His decision-making process, leading to the recall of all forms of Tylenol from every store in the country, has since become a textbook case on company integrity and accountability.

I have a number of philosophies that guide me. I think everybody, in the long run, is motivated by trust. That anything we do – whether we're trying to build an organization or trying to create products and services is guided by the fact that the people who are influenced –

our constituencies – want to trust us. If there is a guiding moral principle in most people's lives, I think it's integrity.

I think that the world is searching for trust in all of their institutions. And I think those that perform the best and continue to perform the best over time, whether they're a parent – a family's an institution as well – or a teacher, or whether they're a business, I think we're all guided by a desire to trust those that we're working with.

As I look back on Tylenol, I think that the only way that we could have done what we did was to have all of the institutions that were affected by the Tylenol poisonings believe in us. And I want to emphasize, believe in us, the company – whether it was the head of the FBI, the FDA, or the people that we spoke to in Congress or at the White House. I look back and realize how quickly the country responded to that issue. It wasn't just what we did. The country had to respond in a myriad of ways. And they responded and listened to our advice because they trusted the institution from which that advice was coming.

There was no lack of trust about Johnson & Johnson. There was no thought that this was something that we were doing that was only in our own self-interest. And that came from a hundred years of experience. While I was the person that had to lead and carry the message to those institutions – and I think they trusted me personally, too – I think they trusted me largely because I represented an institution that had been around for a hundred years and had earned the trust of its entire constituency.

There was a lot of backlash from stockholders, but the

way I managed Johnson & Johnson was consistent with the way I managed the crisis. I always encouraged people to fight back and to argue. I used to call it "creative conflict" – that the more you allowed people to argue out issues, particularly complicated ones, the more creative the group would become because new ideas came forward that wouldn't have come forward without it.

We didn't persuade everybody that we were right, in general, because so many people were involved and because this was being debated publicly. You couldn't turn on the news without seeing it, and you couldn't pick up a newspaper without reading about it.

My belief is that those institutions that survive over time are those that have the better consumer franchise because the consumer, collectively, is smarter than any of us are individually. If they're allowed to speak, and if leadership is listening to them, over time, better decisions will be made and that's what happened to us. We were going out every single day talking to all kinds of people to get their feelings about what we were doing.

Personally, I believed that we could save the product. We were not going to lose the business, but I never envisioned the extraordinarily positive effect on the future of that business because of our behavior. I thought we might save 60-70% of the business, and it's probably fifteen times as big as it was, now. And I think a lot of that was the cumulative sense of trust that the public evidenced by buying our product. I think the experience confirmed my own deep belief that you can do well by doing good. That's a buzzword phrase, but I think it's true. I think that the more we do that's right, the more successful we are as individuals and as institutions.

James Burke is currently Chairman of the Board of Partnership for a Drug-Free America.

THE MORNING OF SEPTEMBER 11, 2001, began, as it did for many, with a phone call. It was a morning that changed everything. Through the hazy numbness of disbelief, we struggled with feelings of shock, outrage, and pain as we watched events unfold in New York, Washington and Pittsburgh.

Matt Zoller Seitz is a reporter for the *Newark Star-Ledger* whose perspective as a film and TV critic took a decidedly personal focus. After September 11th his observations read like dispatches from the front. Although his columns sometimes serve to nudge the media as well as his readers out of their complacency, Seitz is well aware of his own responsibility.

One aspect that consumed so much of my time was explaining the industry to the public – the ego wars, ratings, the who's-hired-who's-fired aspect of the entertainment industry. Ultimately, it wasn't important. The construction of the images is less important than the ideas and emotions that those images generate. I didn't really figure this out until after September 11th. What I *should* be doing is explaining the public to the industry.

I wrote a column about a week after the attack, about

the misuse of images of the towers burning and how they were being shown over and over for no good reason. They would be interviewing an expert on air travel or terrorism or psychology, and they would split the screen, and on one part they'd show the person being interviewed and the other half would show the towers burning! And, this, to me, was obscene. Clearly, they were locked in some kind of mode. I mean, they're all good people. I deal with these people. They're decent, intelligent people who never would've imagined that they were doing something horrible. They were just simply locked in this mode, and they couldn't seem to get out of it. And I wrote a very angry column about it. I wasn't saying anything that the public wasn't already feeling. The important thing is, I was saying what the public was feeling, which is something that everybody in this position should try to do more often.

A few days after that I interviewed Nick Robertson, the CNN correspondent in Afghanistan, and I only had seven minutes to talk to him, so I tried to reprint his answers to my questions in as much detail as I could justify. And I did what I always do at the end of an interview, which is to say, "Is there anything that you would like to add." And he said, "Yes. There is something I'd like to ask your readers. Do you have any idea what the U.S. might have done in other parts of the world in order to make some people there angry enough to kill themselves in order to kill us?" Which is a valid question. But, in placing it at the end of the column, it gave the wrong impression.

It made it seem like this guy was saying we deserved to be attacked in this way, that those people were somehow culpable in their own death. And it made it seem like I condoned that idea, which I didn't. I mean, what reasonable person would? And I got a lot of angry mail about it. Some of it was just furious. There were some people who said that they were particularly upset with me because the columns I'd written up to that point had seemed so on-the-money. They felt that I was representing them and suddenly I had turned on them.

I personally wrote every single person back and explained myself. Then I got Nick Robertson on the phone in Pakistan to do a follow up column the next week and explained to him that the readers were angry and could he please clarify his statements. And he did and so I wrote a follow-up column.

The implication of that quote – and I still thinks it's valid – is that America, generally, has spent way too long feeling as if the rest of the world doesn't really matter, that we have to learn about the rest of the world, that everything we do has an impact. And it's not necessarily the impact we intend. It may end up better than we anticipated. It may end up worse. But we have to understand the impact that we have, and we can't do that if we don't know anything about any other countries except our own. I'm going to write a column very soon, which calls upon the network news divisions to make their interest in world news permanent for reasons of national security because this country will not be secure if we are ignorant of the rest of the world. And it is, I think, very dangerous and destructive to go back to that state of ignorance.

At the age of 26, Thom Mount became the youngest president of Universal Pictures. In the following eight years, he was responsible for the development and production of over 150 motion pictures including *Fast Times at Ridgemount High, The Breakfast Club* and *Coal Miner's Daughter*. In 1984, he founded The Mount Company where he produced such films as *Bull Durham, Tequila Sunrise*, and *Night Falls on Manhattan*. Mount's story reminds us that our moral responsibility can extend to the things we create.

Some years ago, when I was running Universal, we financed and distributed a film called *The Deer Hunter*. At the time we released that picture, several American teenagers emulated the Russian roulette sequence in that movie and died. And I had to face the parents of those dead children who believed, to some degree, that their kids were dead because of this movie.

The death of a child is irreconcilable, and it's very, very hard to say to a parent, and I'm a parent myself, that no one has ever lost a child because a movie made them do something. No kid, who has his or her head screwed on, has ever played Russian roulette. That kind of risk, or any lethal kind of risk inspired by a movie, comes from a failure of the kid to understand where reality ends and fantasy starts.

If you took the position that you would never make any movie that might influence anyone in any way that was negative, you'd never make any movie because everything you do in a movie suggests the possibility of emulation by someone in the public. Out of 280 million Americans, there will be a few people who are impressionable and unbalanced. Very hard for their parents to accept.

The first thing is to try to share in this impossible level of grief. And the second aspect is to try to offer some sense that what has happened here isn't a petty event initiated by one image in a movie, but it's part of a larger fabric of life for those kids now departed and for the rest of us. It's very tough territory. Almost every aspect of our culture is, in some way, wrapped up in or touches on violence and themes of violence. And, that's part of the message you have to extend to the parents because you have to give them some place to go. You can't let them believe that, somehow, the image of the Roulette scene, like a virus, infected them.

I think there's a huge responsibility for filmmakers to not only take a hard look at moral issues, but the moral impact of the films they make. What I try to do in my own pictures is create work that I believe will contribute to the positive evolution of the species or to a positive debate in the culture or a greater understanding of the human condition in all of its colors.

GARY E. JOHNSON was a two-term governor of New Mexico. Prior to becoming governor, Johnson and his wife, Dee, founded

Big J Enterprises, a successful, full-service, commercial and industrial construction company still operating in New Mexico. Throughout his personal and professional life, Governor Johnson has seven principles that remain essential to his decision-making philosophy. His story demonstrates number six: *"Acknowledge mistakes immediately. There may still be time to salvage things or to make corrections. Take Henry Kissinger's advice – 'Anything that will be revealed eventually should be revealed immediately.'"*

In 1994, a reporter calls me and says, "Hey. I have this story that your company faked a piping test out on the Intel job site. What do you know about it?" I said, "I have no idea what you're talking about!" The next morning the headlines in the newspaper read, "BIG J ENTERPRISES FAKES PIPE TEST." So, we're in the airplane at 5:30 in the morning and I pick up the paper and I'll be damned if the story doesn't sound plausible.

I'm on the phone waking up all my key superintendents. "Do you know anything about this? Is this true?" Nobody knows anything. "Find out about it." We take off at 5:30, head to the southern part of the state, and by the time I get there, what they find out is that, yeah, apparently this is true! This is a pipe test that got faked and by the supervisor involved. And, what had transpired between the time I had taken off and landed was this superintendent quits! He doesn't really comment on whether it's true or not, but he quits.

What apparently has happened is exactly as the story is reported. Our concern is, does the pipe have integrity and that we're going to be liable for any problems associated with it. Almost immediately, I am asked, "What's your take on this story?" And my response is, it appears as though the story is true. We're going to find out exactly what has transpired. None of us have any knowledge of what has happened, but individuals that do have knowledge will be held accountable and, of course, we're going to be accountable to the customer.

The next day we get us another headline, "JOHNSON SAYS STORY TRUE!; looking into it; gonna make good by the pipe." We have to spend about thirty thousand dollars on testing this pipe – which is something that we should do. We test the pipe, actually do a re-pressurization of the pipe. In the meantime, these five days are going by – explaining how it should never have been faked in the first place, but the reality of the situation is that these things seal themselves, and sometimes they don't hold these pressure tests, which is not an excuse but this is what motivated the superintendent to actually do it.

Long and short of it, the pipe tests out, 100%. I fessed-up to it from the minute I found out about it, and we were accountable for the whole thing.

JACK SIMS is president and owner of PDMS, Inc., a Texas based company that specializes in retail design and construction and national account light fixture distribution for clients such as Barnes & Noble and Jamba Juice. I first contacted Sims by way of a talk I was preparing to give to a conference held for his industry. He was helpful in discussing issues common in retail construction. When it comes to ethics, Sims explained, "There's not a whole lot of room for philosophy in this business." In the face of an extraordinary financial circumstance, He stood his ground and remained accountable to those his company owed money.

I believe that integrity, honesty, dependability, accountability, and respect for others are critical characteristics for everyone regardless of social or political status. There are no double standards in either private or business life.

The design and construction business is difficult and demanding. Every day is a challenge to stay competitive without forfeiting integrity.

In 1982 I formed my company with a partner (51% and 49% respectively). In 1989, my partner decided to utilize company funds and resources without my knowledge to establish a competing business owned by him and several employees of our company. Needless to say, in addition to the anger from this betrayal, the financial crisis that followed was devastating; over a million dollars owed to subcontractors and suppliers on numerous construction jobs located throughout the United States and the company profit from these projects to pay these debts were lost to my company.

After consulting several accountants and attorneys, the consensus was to file bankruptcy both for the corporation and myself personally, walk away and start over again with a different corporate name. What they really were recommending was for me to cheat multiple innocent parties out of monies they legitimately earned. That maneuver would erase my legal liability and allow me to walk away as though nothing had happened. The fallacy was that their solution included no consideration for the permanent scar that I would carry for the rest of my life, no consideration for my personal reputation in the industry, and no consideration for the damage inflicted on all the creditors. Other than that, it was perfect!

After agonizing over their recommendation, I decided the experts were wrong. My decision was to "do what was right!" We had to be accountable. We had to honor every commitment and pay every debt in full. There was no choice, no decision. The only decision was "how" to do that. I contacted every subcontractor and supplier personally and arranged to pay them over a brief period of time. I confirmed every agreement in writing and thanked them for working with me. I utilized the balance of the line of credit at the bank to pay the debt, negotiated an agreement with the bank to convert that amount into a note, and agreed on a monthly payment and interest rate.

I created a "get well" plan with the assistance of my Chief Financial Officer and solicited the participation of my key employees. We had to operate without a line of credit because there were no more funds available to us at the bank. This was a difficult task, but not impossible.

We launched the plan and I updated the team on our progress on a regular basis. Five years later at a "note burning" dinner party at my house for the key employees, we burned the note from the bank stamped "paid in full $1,339,300.00." Every debt was paid, the bank was paid plus interest, and not a single lawsuit or mechanics lien was filed on a construction project. Most important, our reputation in the industry was intact. We all shared a sense of great self-satisfaction. We "did what was right" rather than what was legally acceptable or what was easy! Today, we are a $10,000,000.00 company with a mission statement that reflects honesty, dependability, accountability and integrity.

SPORTS JOURNALIST FRANK DEFORD'S RESPONSE talks about the importance of self-restraint.

I'm sure that most people of good heart live by the same moral canon – one that changes little over time. However, what has happened recently, in the more sophisticated world we live in, is that while people may be no worse than ever, the ability to slur others is easier come by and more far-reaching.

I have myself been wounded by false accusations, glibly offered, that have quickly moved on, soon broadly disseminated. Especially, then, as a journalist, I forever caution myself to be more sure and understanding before voicing criticism. Nowadays, once the cat is out of the bag, it screeches and scratches, and there is no getting it back, ever.

To be cautious for the sake of others may seem like a

small principle, but one that must be held more dear now. We simply must be more careful in how we speak, for the opportunity to damage the innocent greatly is greater than ever. The larger part of honor now is sensitivity.

ELAINE THOMSEN is a real estate broker in Indian Wells, California. She is past-president of the California Desert Association of Realtors and currently a State Director for the California Association of Realtors. For Thomsen, being responsible includes the necessary self-restraint in advancing your own self-interests at a cost to others.

To be an ethical person is to have the intention that I will have the proper judgment, to react in any situation with a sincerity that is honest and reliable. Granted, we may sometimes be tested in 'a moment of principle.' We may face unusual, volatile, and stressful situations, but for the most part, the test comes everyday in the little things we do and decisions we make. It's the accumulation of the little choices that make us who we are.

Many years ago I faced a situation that changed my life. The CEO of a large corporation offered me an opportunity for a position that few women would have been offered at the time. However, in order to take advantage of the opportunity I would have to betray the trust of a long time friend and co-worker.

The CEO wanted to replace one of our vice-presidents but had no grounds to fire him. The CEO said if I were to "rat" on our vice president, he would have a poor performance review to use against him. I would be named the new vice president in his place and no one would ever know what I had done.

I chose not to betray my friend and refused the position. As a result, the CEO applied unbearable pressure and harassment until I felt I had no choice but to resign. It would have been so easy to accept a prestigious new position with increased income, and my friend would never have been the wiser. The situation called for integrity, fairness, human dignity, friendship, and loyalty to myself and those who depended on me.

The decision to stand by my established principles, to make an unpopular decision, and to accept the consequences of my decision, was not an easy thing to do. Co-workers and friends who knew me well were exasperated with my decision. I couldn't explain and they could not understand what I was doing. When one door closes, another one always opens. It has never failed me. Because I became a free agent when I left my last position, I was offered an opportunity that has put me on a fast track ever since.

My position in the workplace and in the real estate community is a position of leadership. Leadership is a position of respect, and with it comes the obligation to utilize the position to help others.

Hard choices are effortless to make when you have true friends. A true friend is someone who can sing your song back to you when you have forgotten the words. I

always invite my friends to be true to me and sing my song
when I forget the words. It makes reality so much easier
and inescapable.

KARL GROSSMAN teaches investigative journalism at the State
University of New York/College at Old Westbury. His books
include *The Wrong Stuff: The Space Program's Nuclear Threat To
Our Planet* and *Cover-Up: What You Are Not Supposed to Know
About Nuclear Power*. He has also written and narrated investigative documentaries for TV. For his work, Grossman has been honored with the James Aronson Award, John Peter Zenger Award
and George Polk Award. We don't often hear of journalists practicing self-restraint when it comes to investigative stories, which
makes his story all the more compelling.

> I'm an investigative journalist, have been for more than
> three decades, and a basic principle that I live by was
> engraved above the entrance to the *Cleveland Press and
> News* where I first worked as a copyboy: "Give light and
> the people will find their own way." Giving "light" is not
> always an easy matter, journalistically.
>
> In 1985 I learned that NASA intended to launch two
> space shuttles in 1986 with plutonium-fueled space
> probes aboard. What the government finally advised was
> that, yes, there could be serious consequences if the pluto-
> nium – considered the most toxic radioactive substance –
> was dispersed in an accident, but the Department of
> Energy and NASA claimed the risk was "very small due to

the high reliability inherent in the design of the space shuttle." The likelihood of a catastrophic shuttle accident, it was claimed, was but 1-in-100,000.

As a journalism professor, I tell my students that you don't want to scare people with a story unnecessarily, and this is something I practice as a journalist. You have to be very careful. You are exposing, you are revealing, and you have got to make sure that what you have is solid. At 1-in-100,000, the likelihood of a disaster was so small, I thought, how should a journalist report on such a potential catastrophe with such a tiny likelihood? So I kept thinking about the situation, preparing to do some sort of account but wanting to do it properly.

On January 28, 1986, I was on my way to teach my Investigative Reporting class when I heard over the car radio that the *Challenger* had blown up. I stopped at an appliance store and saw that horrible image on 100 TV sets and thought, what if it was May of '86, the date of the *Challenger's* next mission, when it was to have onboard the *Ulysses* plutonium-fueled space probe with 24.2 pounds of plutonium? Instead of seven astronauts dying many, many more people could have died if the plutonium was dispersed in the explosion.

I kept asking why? Why use nuclear materials on space devices? The plutonium on other space probes is used not for propulsion but just to generate a small amount of electricity to power onboard instruments. Why not use solar, photovoltaic energy? Why put the entire space program at risk by using nuclear material?

I discovered that General Electric, which manufactured the plutonium systems, and Lockheed Martin, which took over that division of GE, long lobbied the government to use their plutonium systems in space. Further, Los Alamos and Oak Ridge National Labs, involved in developing nuclear systems for space, were seeking to retain and expand their funding. Then I got to the military connection. The U.S. military wants nuclear-powered weapons in space. That's been a key reason why NASA has been insisting on using nuclear power in space even when solar power would suffice. After the end of the moon missions and seeing its budget drop, NASA became increasingly involved with the military.

The problem is that public relations at NASA, DOE, and GE were trying to engineer public consent. Public relations, defined by Edward Bernays who claimed to be the founder of the field, is "engineering public consent." That diametrically opposes what I believe in. What I believe is, get the information out! Let the chips fall where they may.

These PR people and scientists had lied to me, to the rest of the United States and to the world, on these numbers. In fact, the famous physicist, Richard Feynman, when he investigated the *Challenger* accident, as a member of the presidential commission, was outraged. "NASA owes it to the citizens, from whom it asks support, to be frank, honest and informative so that these citizens can make the wisest decisions for the uses of their limited resources. For successful technology, reality must take precedence over public relations. The nature cannot be fooled."

THIS IDEA OF SELF-RESTRAINT AND RESPONSIBILITY in the press is a debate that often comes up. During the summer of 2001, the media's coverage of Congressman Gary Condit's relationship with missing intern, Chandra Levy, raised questions about the standards and responsibility of the press. I explored these questions with *Newsweek* senior editor, columnist, and contributor, Jonathan Alter during that media frenzy.

The idealistic and principal purpose of journalism is to shine a light in dark corners and provide not just information but knowledge and education for citizens so that they can use that information and act on it. But journalism is also a business. If you didn't have a way to pay the bills, you couldn't do good journalism. So the purpose of journalism is, to my mind, secondarily, to make money because if it doesn't make money, it doesn't exist.

For me, there's no firm standard because journalism is not a science, and fortunately, it's not a business with inflexible standards. It very much depends on the situation. Gary Condit's private life would be of no journalistic interest, nor should it be, if the young woman hadn't been missing. I could tell you of many people that I've known on Capitol Hill and heard rumors that they were having affairs, and I haven't checked out any of them. But, if they were related to a possible murder, then that would be a different story.

WHAT DO YOU STAND FOR?

Now, just because I believe that the Gary Condit story deserved some coverage doesn't mean I believe it should have been covered day and night. So, I think the media lost some proportion on it.

One of the problems with a lot of the cable coverage of the Condit business is that it didn't "advance the ball" and was filling airtime without bringing anything new. At *Newsweek*, the stories that we did on the Condit/Levy matter all advanced the story. And, if it did not advance the story in some fashion, we didn't do it.

However, when you have 24-hour cable and people are lapping it up, you have a strong inclination to want to give them more of it even if you don't have anything new to report. And that's when news values get corrupted because they are going on the air with nothing more to say. At that point they're moving from journalism to pandering, marketing, and promotion.

Journalism has become so much more commercial and so much more market-oriented in recent years that it's in danger of being seen as just another business. It *is* a business, but it shouldn't be just another business. When that happens it becomes much more difficult to carve out first amendment protections.

I think that journalists have to fight to do stories that are important, fight to make sure that stories are not being hyped or blown out proportion, and fight internally for the right kind of journalism. Most people in the business do have the right intentions. They're really not cynical or they wouldn't be journalists. You can *pose* as being cynical, but you can't really *be* cynical and get up every morning and do what's required to be a reporter.

Obviously some sources are more reliable than others. *Newsweek* is more reliable than *The Drudge Report* or *The National Enquirer.* But there are other occasions where, because they care less about accuracy, those publications might get a story first. So, sometimes journalists have to be willing to sacrifice a little bit of timeliness for accuracy, and that's always a difficult challenge. And it has to be compelling. That's a requirement of journalism as well. It's not enough to say, "Eat your peas." It needs to benefit from great storytelling. A good story is a mixture of fresh reporting and smart analysis of what's wrong, and also right, with a person or an institution.

What I try to do is give context to things. And I think that's an important part of journalism that is, in the press of events and on deadline, often forgotten.

9

areté

T HE GREEKS CALLED IT *ARETÉ*.

Traditionally translated as "virtue," its central meaning is excellence. In the *Iliad* and the *Odyssey*, *areté* is applied to courage and strength, especially when exhibited in competition, and this is one common dimension. But it's more.

The third aspect of responsibility, the pursuit of excellence, carries an ethical component when others count on our effectiveness at a given task. Striving for excellence not only requires doing's one's best, but acting diligently, and persevering in overcoming obstacles, as well as demonstrating a commitment to improve our knowledge, skills, and judgment when it comes to carrying out our responsibilities.

"The quality of a person's life," the great football coach Vince Lombardi once said, "is in direct proportion to their commitment to excellence, regardless of their chosen field of endeavor."

Bɪʟ Keane writes about the warm, funny, personal moments in family life. And he succeeds through the poetry of a comic. Today, *The Family Circus* is the most widely syndicated daily comic panel in the world, appearing in 1,500 newspapers. The more I re-read his response the more I could relate to the challenge and value for each of us to persevere with an idea or goal and remain true to our *best* self in the process.

> The prime principle I live by is "Be Yourself." This is particularly true in the creative field. You cannot "fake it" and remain undetected. Throughout my 50 years in the cartoon profession I have met many, many successful people, and the one quality that is evident in everyone is *Persistence*. Never give up on an idea or project in which you believe. Stick-to-itiveness is the key.
>
> In high school I was inspired by the top cartoonists of that time and taught myself to draw by methodically copying their published works (mostly *The New Yorker* magazine cartoonists) until I developed my own style. With persistence a fledgling in any field eventually emerges from

the cocoon with the confidence necessary to "Be Yourself."

RANDY ATAIDE is president and shareholder in two affiliated companies, Mountain View Fruit Sales and Mountain View Cold Storage in Reedley, California. He is engaged in the business of storing, selling, and shipping fruit – peaches, plums, nectarines, apricots. His story not only demonstrates doing one's best, but the necessary diligence in finding the truth in resolving a difficult situation.

For several years now, we have had less than ideal growing conditions for crops. In the 1997 harvest season, during a huge crop of fresh table grapes, I had a mid-sized storage customer who had greatly increased his volume. This customer, "Acme," decided that some of its grapes would be held in long-term storage for the later, fresh market season.

We watch these grapes a bit closer, but the biological reality is once you cut a bunch of grapes off a vine, it is in the process of dying, and the very best I can do in storage is to slow the deterioration down. In ideal conditions, one can get up to ninety days storage life out of a box of grapes. During the 1996-97 season, growing conditions were less than ideal.

About five weeks into storage, Acme began to notice a change in the condition of the grapes. The problem was entirely random; many boxes would look fine, but then an occasional box would have some slight discolored berries, some minor breakdown of tissue, etc. Acme called in a plant physiologist, or in the words of the trade, a "hired gun." After review he concluded that the grapes had suffered some slight freeze damage, but he was puzzled by the lack of other symptoms.

Freeze damage in grapes or most produce is fairly clear and has well-defined symptoms. Also, freeze damage shows up near the vent holes in the grape box, as this is where the too cold air would pass through the box. This was not the case in Acme's grapes. All equipment in the cold storage had operated properly and had not shown any evidence of a freezing event. At the time of the alleged freeze, I was storing for a total of eighteen customers, involving well over one hundred growers, and no one else was complaining of a problem. If we froze grapes, it was inevitable that some other product would be injured as well. Now what?

The principles that I stand upon are Christian in their origin and nature. Having said this, I would suppose that many in business in America would say the same, so then why is there so much conflict if Christ calls us to a higher standard of reconciliation, justice and fairness? In this situation, where then do I "hang my hat?"

I consider the following:

1. *"Always think the best of your customers, but don't be naïve."* This is giving someone the benefit of the doubt. If there is not clear and convincing evidence that the business is in the right, do all you can to assist the customer.

2. *"Be slow to speak, quick to listen and slow to anger."* In one meeting I was personally sworn at and had my character

WHAT DO YOU STAND FOR?

disparaged by the principals of Acme in front of several of my managers and vendors. My instincts were to challenge back and raise my voice, but I did not give in to the temptation.

3. *"Do your homework."* We sought the counsel of three University of California experts – a plant physiologist, a viticulturist, and a County Farm Advisor from the University of California – with years of experience in diagnosing freeze damage. All independently concurred that what Acme was seeing was the ordinary breaking down of grapes at the end of their shelf life, not freeze damage. A private "hired gun" I retained also concluded the same and produced an excellent report. All of this was to prepare for the litigation I knew was coming, as I had refused to honor Acme's demand for over $200,000 in alleged damages.

4. *"Always seek the truth no matter how painful."* People make mistakes, employees can fail. Could a staff member have done something wrong to cause harm or to sabotage Acme's grapes? Nothing showed up.

5. *"Grow from the difficult times."* I took this experience to implement a multitude of procedures to watch things more carefully and respond with data and materials if a question ever came up in the future.

6. *"Draw counsel from a few advisors."* Living in a small agricultural community, the dispute between Acme and Mountain View was well known. To voice my opinion loudly and

assertively would not serve my family, my business or myself well. However, a pastor told me some years ago that when you are personally attacked, let others who know you well come to your defense. It took all the self-discipline I had to implement his advice, but it was the right advice.

After three and a half days of depositions, Acme's Sales Manager and V.P. literally caved and the suit was dismissed. Not only a dismissal, but a written agreement whereby Acme admits that they were wrong in their diagnosis; that if they tell others anything else they could be liable for damages; that Acme would receive no financial compensation or damages for their claim; and related clauses to protect Mountain View's reputation. It was an expensive but sweet victory.

In the fall of 2000, I was surprised at my office by my adversary in the Acme dispute. He asked if he could speak with me, and I welcomed him in. He proceeded to compliment me for the business my partners and I had built and to apologize for what had occurred. "I know that I will need to stand before God some day and answer honestly for what happened. I knew it was wrong, and I wasn't man enough to put a stop to it. Will you forgive me?" I accepted his apology and verbalized the forgiveness that I had long ago done. We then resolved to take some steps in the future to continue to heal the rift between our two companies.

WHEN I WAS GROWING UP the "King of the Cowboys" was Roy

WHAT DO YOU STAND FOR?

Rogers. He was as quick with a friendly word and smile as he was with the necessary grit in handling tricky situations. He was also the snappiest dresser of all the cowboys. Roy was part of a time when gallantry and good deeds were something that we all tuned in to watch on a weekly basis. The only thing was...Roy was a "TV" cowboy.

Nowadays, *real* cowboys display the kind of grit that comes from sitting on top of a bull for what seems like the longest eight seconds you'd ever want to face. Ty Murray was the Tiger Woods-Michael Jordan of his sport with a record seven Professional Rodeo Cowboys Association World All-Around Championship titles. *And* he has the same winning smile and approachable nature of Roy in pursuit of his own standard of excellence.

I stand for never settling for less than the very best I can do.

At the 1993 National Finals Rodeo my 5th go-round bull fell down when he was leaving the chute. He got back up and bucked okay.

I had fourth place in the go-round won, but I got the option of a re-ride. Everyone thought I shouldn't take the re-ride because the caliber of bulls at the NFR stands a good chance of throwing you off. I told them I didn't come here to win 4th, I came to win 1st. I took the re-ride and ended up 2nd in the go-round. That year I ended up winning the World Championship by $95.00. Had I not taken that re-ride I would have been the *reserve* World Champion.

BESIDES BEING A WORLD-CLASS DECATHLETE, SAM ADAMS has served as the meet manager for the decathlon and heptathlon in the 1984 Olympic Games in Los Angeles as well as a number of meets between the United States and Russia and the United States and other European teams.

When basketball coach Bobby Knight was fired from Indiana University, Adams was offended that any coach with an attitude such as Knight's would have kept his job that long. His response expresses what many believe to be an important goal in sports education: a commitment to continuous improvement and doing one's best with the available resources.

My athletic background has had a strong influence on my life. Brutus Hamilton was my track and field coach while I was a student at UC Berkeley. He was much more than a coach. For me, he was an inspiration. His team was his family, and we were proud to be thought of as such. Brutus had a saying, "My boys stay coached." He taught us how to win and what to do when you lose. More importantly, he would teach you how to be a real person in life.

I have competed at relatively high levels including two Olympic trials in track and field: the javelin throw and the decathlon. In the decathlon, I was in the top five twice. Competing in these events taught me a lot. I learned that winning is not everything and that satisfaction does not need a "win" to be satisfying.

I feel very strongly that in my realm we need a code of ethics. And more importantly, follow it. At present, we have a situation where the most important thing for an individual is to 'win, be the best.' But, because of obvious limitations, this can only be achieved by a limited number of people. In my opinion, the most important thing and the principal goal I have attempted to foster in all the athletes I have worked with is to do your very best. Individual achievement is a precious goal.

My 'moment of principle' occurs every time I talk to my team or any member of it. I try to follow the principle: do your very best. This is not a goal that you attempt without thought. What is "very best"? It is a goal that is achieved by work, study, and understanding and, most of all, a love of what you are achieving and doing without the use of illegal substances.

My purpose in working with these kids is threefold. I want to help them enjoy what they are doing, build confidence in their knowledge of the mechanics of the events, and understand that taking second or third is not losing.

Any person who accepts the challenge and enjoys the effort and the lifts from competition is not a loser. The loser is one who quits because he or she cannot win.

ONCE UPON A TIME...before Rush Limbaugh, Howard Stern, and G. Gordon Liddy, there existed an Emerald City of imagination called radio. *The Lone Ranger*, *Green Hornet*, and *Sergeant Preston of the Yukon* were just a few of the programs created and broadcast from WXYZ in Detroit. It was the launching ground for talents like Mike Wallace, Soupy Sales, Danny Thomas and Dick Osgood.

Osgood went from New York theater to work in network radio and success as a broadcaster, writer and researcher. A year before his own death, His responsibilities focused on three important objectives in his life.

> At 90, I found myself with three purposes in life: 1) to take care of my wife, 2) to not be a burden to anybody, and 3) to set an example for my children and six grandchildren. To help me, I inaugurated two periods of prayer & meditation, daily – at 8 a.m. and 5 p.m. – combining Jewish, Christian, and Hindu faiths in my mantra or affirmation.
>
> The first ended at 2:15 a.m., May 22, 1999, when my precious wife died after thirteen months of pain and steady physical deterioration. During that time, I did everything possible – laundry, getting meals, making beds, house work, yard work, grocery shopping, banking and dressing infections. I got her up at 9:30 or 10:00 a.m. and was kept busy until I got her to bed at 10 p.m. Meditation, prayer, and love gave me what I needed to do what had to be done.
>
> What do I stand for? What principles have I lived by? What I wrote in the first paragraph of this letter. These principles were put to the supreme test from late March 1998 to May 22, 1999. I lived in the spirit with God. I did what was right without attachment to results. I try to connect with the infinite spirit within.

MAJOR GENERAL DONALD GARDNER (USMC Retired) was awarded the Silver Star for demonstrating uncommon courage under heavy enemy fire and preserving the integrity of his unit after being wounded by an enemy grenade.

When I shared the text of his citation with John Baldwin –

another contributor who served in the same conflict – he was quick to point out just how significant this truly was. "Not only are few Silver Stars awarded," Baldwin told me, "but in the Corps, it is *expected* that a Marine go beyond the bounds of mere soldiers."

Of the eleven leadership principles Gardner cites as important to Marines, two reflected his steadfastness in doing one's best and setting an example.

In 1996, I became the President and Chief Executive Officer of the Intrepid-Sea-Air-Space Museum. *Intrepid* was a monument to the more than 200 young Americans who lost their lives during World War II and the Intrepid's active service in that conflict.

The task of getting the ship on a business footing meant holding people responsible and leading with discipline and compassion, yet firmness. One of the requirements to become a business was to update the labor contracts. This led to some very intense labor contract negotiations. One evening in 1988, I received a telephone call from two very angry people, advising me that, "He works on a ship near the water. Ships can be dangerous places. He could end up in the water." This call came shortly after a most difficult and intense contract negotiation with the International Longshoremen. The comments were meant to convey a threat of bodily harm.

Due to my Marine Corps training, it was not threatening, and, in fact, I was more determined than ever. The negotiations continued without break, and the fair, equitable working conditions I sought were finally achieved.

When I departed *Intrepid*, this same union presented me with a pocket watch inscribed with the words, "Your time here made a difference." I treasure that watch and my time on *Intrepid*. Today, this special ship continues to tell her story to millions of Americans.

I drew on moral strength to make decisions as a Marine and senior commander. These decisions involved combat, Washington as well as the field. In fact, the process is life long. One cannot deal with what life brings your way without character, and it must be consistent with your own behavior if you are to have credibility.

General Gardner currently serves as the Chief Executive Officer, Marine Corps University Foundation in Quantico, Virginia.

INTERNATIONAL INVESTMENT COUNSELOR Sir John Marks Templeton founded one of the largest and most successful investment funds, the Templeton Growth Fund. Among his many philanthropic accomplishments are the John Templeton Foundation and The Templeton Prize. The purpose of the prize is to recognize and honor those individuals who have helped advance the world's understanding of spirituality.

In 1987, Sir John created the Laws of Life essay contest (lawsoflife.org) for his hometown of Winchester, Tennessee. His vision was to encourage young people to reflect and write about the core values that will guide them, whatever they do or wherever they go in life. Since the first contest was launched, the program has spread to thirty-two countries. In 2001, more than 75,000 young people participated in the essay contest. Held in local schools and sponsored by a variety of individuals and groups within each community, the contest offers community members and educators an opportunity to collaborate on a positive activity that benefits young people, schools, and the entire community.

Leisha Slaughter is a 16-year-old from New Jersey whose Laws of Life essay reflects her desire to be her best.

When I was born, as with all people, my life's possibilities were endless. Of course, as with most, down the road there was opposition. However, mine was to be on the inside: I was born deformed, different. A minor error in my leg would lead to much chaos in my early childhood. Troubles mounted on the outside world with my parent's divorce and the illness of my little brother. As these things died down, others arose.

When I started my 6th grade year, I was very optimistic. I was used to starting over, and, as such, I wasn't worried about fitting in or making friends. But despite my views and confidence, I was walking into a superficial reality, a reality that was based on popularity, money, appearance, clothes, power, attitude.

After a month I managed only one friend because most kids chose not to associate with someone like me. One day, I discovered just what the so-called "someone like me" meant. I was walking down the halls to class only to hear laughter followed by talking. Those who were talking weren't aware I could hear them. They laughed at my clothes because they weren't name brand (name brand meant money), and they laughed at my hair because it wasn't as straight as theirs.

This hurt me deeply because I didn't understand why those things would matter, but what hurt more was the fact that almost everyone behaved this way towards me. As for my grades, they remained steady as I continually made the Honor Roll, and because of this many of my peers felt I was an easy target for "aided" cheating. However, this wasn't true and that added to the previous resentments.

The out-casting kept up long into 8th grade, and though I made a few more friends, their attitude hadn't changed. There was one change, puberty and the need for attention from a member of the opposite sex. However, my appearance offset the boys who had been taught to like girls with very pretty faces, large breasts, and a rear to match. Not to mention the added trait of being "easy." As for the girls, many resented my virginity (which is still intact, I'm proud to say), and my intellect.

These insults, actions, and reactions weren't easy to cope with. There were times when I broke down and cried, but I never let it get me down. I found role models in my mom and in *Rashel Jordan*, a character in the book *Night-world*, and in my favorite show *SailorMoon*. They were strong and compassionate women who persevered in adversity. They were examples of success and images of hope. Once I had my stronghold, I set my goals and moved on.

These factors contributed to my law #6: "*It is important to love yourself, because you're the one who has to look yourself in the mirror. Make sure the reflection is one you're proud of."*

In discovering this truth I set out to make sure that I wasn't anything like those who had excluded me. I never wanted to be that kind of person, and in that decision I chose to be someone I would be proud of. And I chose to be true to that person, someone real, the person inside.

I developed my own sense of style, which I based on what I liked rather than how much it cost or whose name was on it. I changed my hair and wore it naturally. Later I joined the choir. It proved to raise my self-esteem. I kept up my grades and ignored the negative insults. I persisted in these things and found many blessings. As a result, I'm graduating in three years. I was a co-star in the school play of *Purlie*, and was accepted to the University of Tampa and their Honor Program. On a more personal note, I am dating a guy who accepts me the way I am.

Since I have acquired these life lessons, I have found it easier to deal with the struggles I face everyday. They have helped me to accept, understand, and know myself better. They have given me the gift of being able to look at someone very special everyday...my reflection.

How do you balance living up to the expectations of others with being true to yourself? How do you find the strength to stand up for what you believe is your own path? These are some of the themes driving the Disney animated feature, *Mulan*. Based on Chinese legend, *Mulan* tells the story of a young girl determined to save her ailing father's life by taking his place when he is called to war. It's as much about honoring the life you have chosen as it is about living an honorable life.

Rita Hsiao, one of the screenwriters, reveals more than a casual similarity to the character she helped shape.

What made the story of *Mulan* interesting to me was its emphasis on duty, honor, and respect – all very important in Asian culture. Mulan's fight was more than on the bat-tlefield. She fought to figure out who she was in this very strong culture. Was she the perfect daughter, the perfect bride? Both were ways to honor and show respect for her parents. Mulan did end up bringing them honor, but in her own way. It was that journey – to do what she felt was right and, in the process, be true to herself – that con-nected with me.

In college, I majored in Artificial Intelligence mostly to please my parents. My true passion was writing. I wrote musicals and plays, mostly to please myself. My parents kept saying I'd never find a job, so I took all these com-puter courses, even though I knew this wasn't what I wanted to spend my life doing. When I graduated, I got my foot in the entertainment door answering phones at a TV production company, which, of course, freaked my parents out. "You just finished school and have this degree and you're answering telephones?" But it was about find-ing the strength to break away and do my own thing.

This came out in *Mulan* in the sense that we wanted her to be strong, to become a woman who was more than what society and her parents expected. Ultimately, Mulan finds strength and conviction where most would find defeat. In the scene after she's been discovered and thrown out of the army for being a woman, she feels horrible. Looking at the helmet she once wore as a warrior, she comes to the conclusion that maybe she didn't go *only* to save her father's life, but also to prove that she could do things right; so that when she looked in the mirror, she'd see someone worthwhile.

I think all of us, at times, are filled with doubt. We hear people tell us, "You can't do that. You should do this." Yet, there's something deep inside all of us that says, "You know what? There's more to me than what you're saying," and then going out and actually trying to prove it to yourself and others.

When I told my parents that I was going to be a screenwriter, my Mom said, "A writer! Will you have health insurance?" Part of the reason I moved out to the West Coast was because I grew up in New York and just wanted to get away and be my own person, figure things out for myself.

Like Mulan, I was torn between wanting to please my parents and wanting to be true to myself – to find that inner strength to stand up for what I wanted. Believing in yourself is very hard when you've got so many external forces telling you how to act or be. But I will always appreciate having been instilled with a strong set of values. Whether it's being respectful of other people, working really hard, or trying to be honest and treating others as you'd want to be treated yourself.

For my birthday, I got a card from my Mom and it was a *Mulan* card. Inside, it read, "The greatest honor is having you for a daughter." I thought, "Hey, my line is in a birthday card that my parents sent to me because they're so proud." It was surreal and touching.

In the early '70s I became transfixed by a dome of white granite sliced almost perfectly in half rising 4,800 feet from the floor of Yosemite Valley. My quest was to not only climb this thing but to film it at the same time. So I drove to a climbing shop in L.A. and over the next few months studied and learned everything I could. And I rock climbed – Stony Point, Joshua Tree, and an oddly shaped stack of granite known as Suicide Rock. I then drove into the Valley, walked to the base of Half Dome, looked up, nodded my head, turned, and left – completely overwhelmed.

Royal Robbins, on the other hand, did not allow his fear to keep him off the granite faces that ringed the valley floor. Whenever climbers spoke of the Valley, they spoke of Royal Robbins.

Two principles have guided many of the important decisions of my life: Integrity and Love. Integrity is being true to yourself. Your character is like something you are sculpting your entire life. Every time you do something that is not "integrated," that splits you up and makes you less "whole." It's like taking a chisel and defacing the statue of the character you have been building. Love is simply the most powerful force in the Universe; it is what holds the

What Do You Stand For?

universe together. Things go better when we let Love guide our actions.

I used to work in a bank. I liked my job! I had interesting work, friends, a good social life, good pay, and security. Then, when I went climbing on weekends, I realized I loved climbing. I was spending five days of seven doing what I liked and two days doing what I loved. Why not do what you love all of the time? Why not indeed? Risky, uncertain, adventurous? Yes!

So I left the bank to devote myself to a life of outdoor adventure. I didn't know where the money was going to come from. I didn't know about marriage or family or sickness or old age. I just had the faith that if I did what I loved, everything else would fall into place around that centralizing principle. And so it has.

ART HARMON volunteered for the Army Air Corps while in high school. His training ultimately resulted in an assignment as a pilot with the legendary Tuskegee Airmen. While attending Pepperdine College in California, Lt. Harmon was recalled to active duty during the Korean conflict where he saw duty in the Strategic Air Command, Far East Air Force and other assignments. As a member of the San Francisco Bay Chapter of the Tuskegee Airmen, Inc., Colonel Harmon currently works on a variety of projects to help "at risk" kids. His response focuses on the importance of perseverance.

One principle that has been a guiding light, almost an

obsession – the no compromise position I have adhered to for as long as I can remember – is to respect the dignity of others regardless of my relationship with them. The difficulty of applying that principle in every situation is apparent but I think that the formula for successful interaction throughout a lifetime depends upon your ability to access each encounter based on your acknowledgement of worth regardless of a conflict of ideas.

As an African-American, I am tested almost daily on my principle. However, I have found strength, not by turning the other cheek, but by stubborn determination to achieve in spite of obstacles, real or imagined.

As a young aviation cadet in Macon County, Alabama in 1943, I was made aware of a local sheriff whose hatred of Negroes was legendary. As long as we confined our activities to the campus, we were fine. But, as soon as you went off campus, you could feel the atmosphere change. When the sun went down, you best be either on campus or on the military installation someplace. There were indications of harassment and beatings if you were out after dark.

I think it's important to set goals for yourself. At the time, my goal was graduating from aviation school. If the obstacle is a sheriff in a local town, I avoid the sheriff. I won't confront him because he's not part of my goal. So, I try to eliminate that obstacle by avoiding it.

DR. ALVIN F. POUSSAINT is the Director of the Media Center at the Judge Baker Children's Center in Boston and one of the nation's leading psychiatrists. He is also a Professor of Psychiatry at Harvard Medical School. A highly regarded specialist on race relations in America, Dr. Poussaint has served as a consultant to many corporations and government agencies. He has lectured and written on a wide range of social issues including the need for tolerance. His story stresses a dedication to hard work, sound judgment, and perseverance to pull you through fearful times.

The core principles in my life are to work hard to achieve my goals and always maintain a high level of commitment and integrity. Never quit. During difficult times, I always said to myself that if I'm going to fail, I'm going to go down fighting. One of my primary goals has been to fight for justice and an end to racial discrimination. I would not, however, let race become an obstacle to my success.

During my work in the civil rights movement, there were many terrifying moments. There was only one, however, when my knees were literally shaking. On June 21, 1966, the second anniversary of the death of three civil rights workers – James Chaney, Andrew Goodman, and Michael Schwerner – Reverend Martin Luther King led a group of us from the Meredith March to the courthouse in Philadelphia, Mississippi. King wanted to pay tribute to these workers who had been killed in Philadelphia.

Andy Young had asked me to walk next to King because I was the physician on the march and had the medical supplies to tend to King if anything happened. We were afraid something would happen because it was a very dangerous situation. The crowd of white townspeople was out of control, shouting and taunting at the marchers as we walked through the town.

Sheriff Rainey and Deputy Sheriff Price, who had been implicated in the murder of the three workers, came out of the courthouse with their weapons and stopped King. Price or Rainey told King he could not proceed. As he stared at Rainey for a long moment, I thought King would keep going and we would all be injured or perhaps killed. Instead, King knelt down and said for everyone to kneel. He said a prayer to honor the three dead workers, then got up and turned around to leave. I was very relieved. Going back to the cars to return to the Meredith march was still frightening. A car driven by a group of white men almost hit Stokely Carmichael; he had to jump out of the way as the car drove straight into the marchers.

In spite of my fear during this incident, I stayed with King and fulfilled what I felt was my duty and commitment to struggle for the rights of African Americans. I served as the Southern Field Director of the Medical Committee for Human Rights from 1965 to 1967 in Jackson, Mississippi. That choice set the course for my life since then.

PATRICIA HILL BURNETT has led an extraordinary life. She was Miss Michigan in 1942 and first runner-up to Miss America that year. She also played the female lead for five years in *The Lone Ranger* and *Green Hornet* radio shows.

In 1969, Burnett demonstrated her commitment to the women's movement by founding the first chapter of the National Organization for Women (NOW) in Michigan, and she went on to join the national board in 1971. She fought hard and long for her cause and remains an active member in many organizations. As if that wasn't enough, she has distinguished herself as a world-renowned painter with portraits of Indira Gandhi, Margaret Thatcher, Rosa Parks, and feminist Betty Friedan. Burnett makes clear that doing one's best with an unpopular task can strengthen character.

I attended a meeting of an organization that was beginning to acquire a very large staff and handle a lot of money. I was sitting in at a meeting, and they said, "We're trying to research how our different local groups are reacting. Are they happy with their membership because we've heard a few grumbles and would anybody like to head up the task force?"

I raised my hand. "Pick out your committee and do it," they said. So I picked eight people, sent out a questionnaire, and, to my astonishment, the answers came back from the different sections who were really getting upset with an organization that wasn't paying any attention to them. They were feeling that the management was sort of elite and spoke only to themselves and kept re-electing themselves. The staff was very good at getting grants and so forth, so they had a great deal of power. Well, the staff heard about it and said, "We want to see this questionnaire, and we don't want you to send *anything* else out until we check it first." So, I sent them a copy and kept them clued in all along.

The time was approaching to give the report to all the

different sections and the members kept saying, "Patricia, it's something that we want to say. Go ahead and give it." So, I went to the committee meeting and, lo and behold, instead of three members there were sixty! It's very interesting to see the way that Parliamentary Law and lawyerly attempts can prevent a report from being given. There were frequent interruptions, and stalling until there was only fifteen minutes left on the agenda. I put my hand up and said, "I have to give this report. I want these last fifteen minutes." They were astonished because I'd always been a very mild-mannered, artistic-type.

In spite of the staff and Board trying to interrupt me, I gave the report. One of the members, who was the smartest of all the lawyers there, came up to me afterward and said, "Patricia, you are so polite, so ladylike, but you cut them off at the knees," which I thought was the most treasured compliment I'd ever received! All of a sudden, to my astonishment, I'm their heroine. People from all over the country talked about my report and what should be done about it. I have a firm course of action and it's under way.

I was in the fortunate position that I had no secret agenda. I was just determined to give that report even though I realized that I'd lost maybe a quarter of them as friends and probably would never get them back. This has happened to me several times in my life. I felt that I had tackled an unpleasant, unpopular job. And I think, even in the smallest thing, if we can force ourselves to approach an unpleasant task and, by God, *do it* no matter how many people are trying to stop you, or how *few* people are watching, then it gives you a self-satisfaction that shows that you have character.

MARGARET KING, PH.D., is director of Cultural Studies & Analysis, a Philadelphia think tank that studies human dynamics, values, and decision making. Her research areas range from theme parks, museums, the popular arts, film, television, cross-cultural issues, and marketing to consumer psychology, decision-making, and culture theory.

King's response reminds us that sometimes excellence means standing up for yourself.

Ethics (as opposed to morals) always implies the context and understanding of the big picture, cause-and-effect relationships, and the fact that you can't change just one thing without a ripple effect system-wide.

I believe that, for many people, there is no single defining 'moment of principle' that sharply illuminates one's character. Instead, we face something far more difficult: a constant barrage of small challenges to ethical standards in which the simplest solution is to just let them go without contest.

As a case in point, I recently opened a newly published book by a colleague of long standing only to discover that two of the chapters credited to this author were – word for word – ones I had written early in my career. What's more, a careful reading of the book has convinced me that many, if not all, of the other chapters were lifted whole or in part from papers delivered at a conference organized by the plagiarist back in the 1970s.

As I said, the "author" was a colleague of long standing. The works of mine that he appropriated were early ones and not critical to my current life and career. It is an academic publication, so there is no issue of his profiting financially from my work. On the other hand, to raise the issue publicly means denouncing someone I considered a friend. To prove my case in full to the publisher means dedicating time, money, and effort that would be better spent on things and people I consider of far more immediate importance. In other words, I have nothing most people would consider tangible to gain – and a lot to lose. I did consider "letting it go," but an attorney friend put it most succinctly: "You have to decide how much you are willing to pay to resolve this. You can decide to let it go, but it's going to cost you in peace of mind. If you can afford that, then do it."

There really is no escape from taking ethical positions, since the decision to do nothing is in itself a decision. Applying an ethical standard requires understanding not only who you are, but also who you want to be. I'm now engaged in a conflict I neither sought nor wanted. My friend was right on target. I can't afford to do anything else.

Consequences of my 'moment': a giant headache for me, for my business partner, for the publisher, and the plagiarist. Currently the publisher is trying to stall any action by asking the perpetrator of this crime if he's done anything wrong: the answer, of course, is no. They don't want to take action: it's inconvenient, expensive, and time-consuming. But now that they've been put on notice, they must think about consequences. Colleagues are supportive but really don't want to get involved. I don't blame them. Except that this case involves defense of authorship, the basic coin of academic achievement.

Ethical Principle: "You don't give up what's valuable about yourself."

ALL THOSE ABOVE THE AGE OF TWENTY-FIVE who do *not* know who Arnold Palmer is, please stand up. That's what I thought. What you may *not* know is that besides being one of golf's iron men, he is also a highly successful business executive, prominent advertising spokesman, skilled aviator, talented golf course designer, and consultant, as well as a devoted father and grandfather. His practical, down-to-earth manner has made him one of the most popular and approachable sports figures in history.

The saga of Arnold Palmer began when he was four years old, swinging his first set of golf clubs, cut down by his father, "Deacon" Palmer, who worked at Latrobe Country Club. Before long, young Palmer was playing well enough to beat the older caddies at the club. The influence his father had on his pursuit of excellence extended beyond the game of golf. The following response comes from both a phone interview and his autobiography, *A Golfer's Life*, written with James Dodson.

I have always felt that you should treat everyone like you'd like to be treated, and I've practiced that with almost everything I do.

My father prided himself on simple, clear logic. He was a very honest man with great integrity and a lot of very heavy feelings about people and how they should be treated. He was a golf course superintendent and a Golf Pro. And he was very protective of the people that worked for him. Sometimes, in country clubs, he would have a situation where maybe the people that are working at the club are not given the same respect that he felt they should.

Not surprisingly, he had the same simple reverence for the rules of the game. The rules were there to be followed because that meant the game would be the same kind of challenge for everybody. He was the man I most admired in the world. He was the man whose hard rules and painful lessons had made me everything I'd become, everything I stood for.

He was as rigid and unyielding on the rules of the game as any USGA official I ever knew, and that's one reason I learned the rules thoroughly at an early age. He preached relentlessly on the importance of replacing divots and repairing pitchmarks, and woe be unto the player – regardless of whether it was his own son or the club president – who failed to treat the golf course with the kind of respect Pap deemed necessary and proper.

He developed even more rigid beliefs about what was right and what was wrong, what a good man did or didn't do. You didn't borrow money. You didn't take what wasn't yours; you didn't lie, cheat, or steal.

What Do You Stand For?

It was also drilled into me that a golf course was a place where character fully reveals itself – both its strengths and its flaws. As a result, I learned early not only to fix my ball marks but also to congratulate an opponent on a good shot, avoid walking ahead of a player preparing to shoot, remain perfectly still when someone else was playing, and a score of other small courtesies that revealed, in my father's mind, one's abiding respect for the game. In a nutshell, Pap had no patience with people who chose to ignore the rules and traditions that made golf the most gentlemanly game on earth.

Pap, in almost every respect, was a modest man, but he burned with a wisdom and intensity about what it took to accomplish great things that were far beyond his own experience. His way of looking at things would prove invaluable to me.

PAP'S RULES

1. A smart man learns early what he does best and keeps on doing it.
2. Be prepared.
3. Stay focused until the job is finished.
4. Respect everyone regardless of their skin color or nationality.
5. Anytime you think you are the best you can be, just remember there is always some guy out there just waiting to beat you. Don't brag about what you've accomplished and don't tell people what you're gonna do – keep your

mouth shut, keep your mind on your own business and show them!

Bob Jones, my first golf hero, once commented that he never learned anything from a golf tournament he won. For better or worse, those moments of unaccountable loss or failure teach us the most about who we are, where we've come from and where we may be headed.

As I've gotten older, I've realized that we need to be constantly challenged to examine ourselves and see what we can give back to this life. I see my primary role as someone who feels a moral obligation to take care of the game that enriched his own life so profoundly, to fuss a little bit when I feel it's necessary, to do whatever it takes to make sure I pass along a game that is in even better shape than I found it.

Hands down, my favorite movie of all time is the one where Spencer Tracy plays a hotshot World War II pilot who flies on instinct and hot coffee. He also has a knack for showboating on every bombing mission he's sent out on until the day comes when he doesn't come back.

The defining moment in *A Guy Named Joe* occurs when he meets Lionel Barrymore, the commanding officer in a place where all good flyers go. Tracy's character has had to learn the hard way the code of the true flier, that "no man is really dead unless he breaks faith with the future and no man is really alive unless he accepts his responsibility to it." Tracy's responsibility, his mission, was not only teaching Van Johnson to fly but inspire him to excellence.

I met Joe Phipps several years ago, first as a new resident to the community where I lived, later as a friend, finally, as a teacher whose extraordinary power changed the way I looked at myself forever.

At a particularly low point in my work, I confided to Joe my frustration with clients who consistently wanted more juice from a lemon that had already been squeezed too much. Joe kindly confronted me with, "Why aren't you working on your own stuff, Jim?" When I recited a litany of excuses, he simply wouldn't accept what he saw as unrealized potential. "You're a writer," Joe told me, "write yourself out of it!" He saw conviction where I saw doubt. He affirmed faith where I felt fear.

Joe was like a spark plug. In his eyes, I saw no uncertainty. In his voice, I heard no hesitation. The energy and conviction with which he spoke inspired me to step outside my fear and "…live up to the best you are capable of and don't try to live up to an impression of how *you* think, or *anyone* else thinks, you should be."

Joe spent so much of his own time helping others realize their excellence, that I never fully understood, until much later, how little time he had left. In his last days of life, he confirmed, once again, for me a courage and commitment to reach for the best inside me.

Joe's strength became my strength. His conviction became my conviction. And that strength and conviction shall remain with me always. As a matter of fact, I like to think that Joe's standing beside me now, like the Spencer Tracy character. Of course, I'm the character with all the potential still trying to get out of my own way. All I have to do is listen. "You know what to do. Now, *do* it. You know who you want to be. Now, *be* it."

10

tikkun olam

"The average citizen must be a good citizen if our republics are to succeed. The stream will not permanently rise higher than the main source; and the main source of national power and national greatness is found in the average citizenship of the nation. Therefore it behooves us to do our best to see that the standard of the average citizen is kept high; and the average can not be kept high unless the standard of the leaders is very much higher."

–THEODORE ROOSEVELT, "Citizenship in a Republic"
from an essay delivered at the Sorbonne, Paris, 1910

IN BOTH WORD AND DEED, Teddy Roosevelt seemed to embody American character. Although only forty-two when he became president, Roosevelt had amassed quite a range of experience as rancher, author, civil service commissioner, naturalist, New York City police commissioner, assistant secretary of the Navy, soldier, statesman and governor of New York.

A proponent of the "strenuous life," Roosevelt's ideas and energy were as boundless as his rhetoric. TR stressed patriotism, responsibility, and civic virtue, and the crowds who heard him speak never doubted what he believed or where he stood on an issue.

Considering recent events both at home and abroad, Roosevelt's words, from an essay entitled "True Americanism" in 1894, seem no less significant today.

"…We Americans have many grave problems to solve, many threatening evils to fight, and many deeds to do, if, as we hope and believe, we have the wisdom, the strength, the courage and the virtue to do them. But we must face facts as they are.

"We must neither surrender ourselves to a foolish optimism, nor succumb to a timid and ignoble pessimism. Our nation is that one among all the nations of the earth which holds in its hands the fate of the coming years. We enjoy exceptional advantages, and are menaced by exceptional dangers; and all signs indicate that we shall either fail greatly or succeed greatly. I firmly believe that we shall succeed; but we must not foolishly blink the dangers by which we are threatened, for that is the way to fail.

"On the contrary, we must soberly set to work to find out all we can about the existence and extent of every evil, must acknowledge it to be such, and must then attack it with unyielding resolution. There are many such evils, and each must be fought after a fashion; yet there is one quality which we must bring to the solution of every problem

WHAT DO YOU STAND FOR?

– that is, an intense and fervid Americanism. We shall never be successful over the dangers that confront us; we shall never achieve true greatness, nor reach the lofty ideal which the founders and preservers of our mighty federal Republic have set before us, unless we are Americans in heart and soul, in spirit and purpose, keenly alive to the responsibility implied in the very name of American, and proud beyond measure of the glorious privilege of bearing it."

Roosevelt spoke often about the value of citizenship and civic virtue. Citizenship means playing by the rules, obeying laws, voting, serving on a jury, reporting crimes, protecting the environment and volunteering time and resources for charitable causes. It means serving your family, community, country and, in a broader sense, the world.

The Hebrew expression *tikkun olam* - repairing the world - is a reminder that each of us has a responsibility to make our world a better place.

WHAT IF YOU COULD GO BACK into our country's past and ask a founding father my question? What would Benjamin Franklin say? How might Thomas Jefferson interpret the principles of the past in a contemporary context?

Franklin and Jefferson offer a unique perspective on civic virtue and citizenship. Many of their principles have been adopted by, or are reflected in the thoughts of, today's leaders. By reviewing their comments – portrayed by historians who can see the relevance in both eras – we can begin to connect current thinking with the timeless values and ethics of American leaders of the past.

Ralph Archbold has been speaking as Benjamin Franklin in talks to corporations and groups around the country for twenty-five years. And all those who have heard him agree that when he speaks, he *is* Ben Franklin!

Talking with Dr. Franklin was like talking to history. He was straightforward and worldly-wise without any of the cynicism that sometimes comes from age, politics or both. But what impressed me most during my time with him was how at ease he made me feel – like an old friend having a conversation on the porch at his home in Philadelphia.

JL: Dr. Franklin, you are a printer, writer, scientist, inventor, philosopher, statesman, founding father… Did I leave anything out?

BF: Oh, a little bit of a rascal, on occasion, I suppose (chuckles)…but that's all rumor so don't pay too much attention to that.

JL: How should I address you, sir?

BF: Are we friends?

JL: I'd like to think so.

BF: Well then, I would say Ben would be fine or Benjamin, if you like.

JL: What do you stand for, Ben? What principles have you lived by?

BF: I begin my day with a daily prayer. "Powerful goodness, bountiful Father, merciful Guide, increase in me that wisdom which discovers my truest interests, strengthen my resolution to perform what that wisdom dictates, and accept my kind offices to thy other children as the only return in my power for the continual good you have given me."

I reflect each morning on what good I might do for someone during that day. And, close each day with the same prayer, reflecting upon whether I had succeeded in doing good for someone during the day.

The noblest question in the world is, what good may I do in it? What will I leave beyond my years that will help someone live a better life, solve a problem, perhaps, accomplish a goal? I've always felt that what we do – in return for the good things that have come to us – is what keeps the good things happening. And I thought that was very important – to treat others honestly…with understanding…not to be contentious, but to be a person who would urge us to discover the noblest goals rather than agitate them into the lower common denominator.

JL: How did you come by these principles?

BF: I really started out, I suppose, as a boy living up in Boston reading *Essays to do Good*. Cotton Mather was a great influence there. My father was very religious, and the bible was a very important part of our family.

I also learned, at a very young age, from the people that were at our dinner table. My father was a soap and candle maker and served the trade of the ships coming into Boston Harbor and would frequently invite guests to our home. I was there to listen and to learn. I read whatever I could and studied.

JL: Can you think of a time in which your convictions were tested?

BF: I remember one particular incident. I was publishing my newspaper, *The Pennsylvania Gazette*, and newspapers were distributed through the mail. And, the man in charge of the post office happened to be my competitor, who also had a newspaper, and he wouldn't carry my papers. And I was very upset about this. I then had the chance to gain the position of postmaster, at a later date, and I had the opportunity at that point to turn the tables and do the same thing to him. And I resisted that temptation.

Regardless of the injury that I had received, I had been trusted with a responsibility, and it was my responsibility to *faithfully* serve in performing that responsibility. And that was part of my philosophy: Where a true friend is the best possession, be a true friend to people.

JL: What do you see as the most important problem facing the country today?

BF: Hmm, I think the most important problem facing the country today is making sure you are passing along the values that are so important to the next generation. Honesty, integrity in dealing with others is very important. Respect others in our home, in our business, in our community. Respect them as individuals.

You see, we talked about taxes, we talked about representation, but what our independence and Declaration of Independence was really about is respect, because that's what we wanted! That's what every person wants. We want to be respected for our talent, energy, our ideas, our intellect. We wanted that same respect from England. We all want this! And so I think it's important that respect for others is the cornerstone of all the values we have. If we don't respect others and ourselves, it won't work.

The great thing that we can do for ourselves and for others is to think about what we are doing *before* we do it, and to think whether we are honoring ourselves, our families, and our God.

To say that Thomas Jefferson was a man of accomplishment is a little like saying the '27 Yankees was a pretty good ball club. What we know of Jefferson the man comes not only from the documents he authored but also from some 20,000 of his letters covering all facets of his business and personal relationships.

Bill Barker has been portraying Thomas Jefferson since 1985 – and beginning in 1993 at Colonial Williamsburg – in an interactive format; that is to say that Jefferson speaks to and answers questions from an audience of adults and children. It is a testimony to Bill's continuing scholarship that when surrounded by school kids who press the historical figure on the tough questions, he engages their hearts and minds by explaining the context of the times while representing the well-mannered nobility of Mr. Jefferson.

JL: At the end of the Declaration of Independence you talk of pledging "…our lives, fortunes, and sacred honor." What do the words "sacred honor" mean to you?

TJ: Sacred honor implies that you've given your word and that you stand behind it. It could imply, perhaps, a great reckoning with fate as to whether you stand or waiver upon your own ground and your own word.

Those of us who signed our names to the Declaration of American Independence recognized that we had our lives, fortunes and property to lose, let alone the lives of those we held dearest to us.

JL: To the question at hand. What do you stand for – what principles have you lived by?

TJ: My principles would be simply, as I wrote in the Declaration – that we may be free to pursue our own lives, our liberty and our happiness. Not to neglect, as well Mr. Locke's other unalienable right in nature, the pursuit of property. Property can be pursuant to happiness, but we should be cautious not to abuse the right of property and use it to neglect, deny and prohibit the happiness, the freedom and the right of others to property.

Accordingly, I believe the most essential freedoms of man are the right to hold an opinion freely and to freely express it; the right to freely assemble in a collective debate over various opinions in an effort to assuage factions and to come to compromise for the common good, and thirdly, the right to petition government for redress of grievances.

JL: It sounds like you are describing what America stands for.

TJ: America stands for the happiness, safety, and liberty of the family of man; for a people who wish to be free to conduct their own lives through a government elected by them as necessary for the preservation of their natural rights. Government should extend itself no further than the elements of protection, that is, protecting individuals from injury by one another but otherwise to leave a people free to pursue their own industry and their own improvement.

JL: Can you describe an example in which your convictions were tested?

TJ: When I was twenty-six years of age, I stood in my first session in the House of Burgesses to second a motion made by Colonel Richard Bland that we receive permission to begin a debate upon ending the importation of slaves to Virginia. That motion was denied.

Slavery had evolved to the extent where we held a wolf by the ear, which we could not let go, let alone hold onto. Our self-preservation, both slave as well as master, was in the one hand while justice was in the other.

But, the debate must be kept open, and we must move forward for the common good in an effort to assuage the great factions amongst us. We can adopt new habits. We can alter our customs. It will not happen overnight. We must look to a higher providence with patience.

JL: As a country, Mr. Jefferson, how can we transcend obstacles such as intolerance and injustice and live up to our highest aspirations?

TJ: Faith is not faith without believing. Let us continue to allow for as much information possible at the public bar. The citizen body may look always to history as an example and as a direction towards where we may be at present and where we may be headed in the future. We must continue to pursue equal and exact justice to all and allow for the decisions of the majority, but the majority must recognize their responsibility to protect the natural rights of the minority.

We should continue to stand behind the freedom of the press and freedom for religion. I think the public debate should always be open; the issues should be continually put before the citizenry; that they have the opportunity to voice their opinion and debate the issues. If it were left to me to decide whether we should have a nation with a government and no newspapers or a nation with newspapers and no government, I should not hesitate a moment but to choose the latter.

"Whom can we trust? Who has the credibility to lead? Are all politicians crooks?" These are just a few of the critical questions Charles Lewis, founder and executive director of The Center for Public Integrity raises in his investigative examination into the inextricable link between Congress and special interests.

"In 1975," Lewis observes, "when the Gallup Organization asked a representative sample of Americans how much confidence they had in Congress, 40% responded: 'A great deal' or 'Quite a lot.' By 1995, only 21% responded that way."

Sometimes we seem so focused on the scandal-of-the-moment that it's not only difficult to sustain strength of character but maintain the necessary faith in elected officials. And yet, there are examples of leaders who do it right. In his 1998 book, *The Buying of the Congress*, Charles Lewis reminds us of two noble examples.

"[Republican John] Williams, a chicken farmer and feed dealer from southern Delaware, had never gone to college. He spoke so quietly on the Senate floor that the news media dubbed him 'Whispering Willie.' But when he spoke, people listened as he exposed the biggest corruption scandals of the late 1940s, 1950s and 1960s – sending hundreds of government officials to prison, saving taxpayers hundreds of millions of dollars – without a sleuthing staff, without the power of subpoena, without a special counsel serving as prosecutor. Congress never appropriated a penny for his investigations, and Williams paid all expenses, such as necessary travel, out of his own pocket. He always informed the subject of an investigation of his findings personally before he announced them publicly, and never once in twenty-four years did he falsely accuse anyone. He also never had a press secretary, something practically unheard of in Washington even then.

"Williams helped uncover wrongdoing by William Boyle, the chairman of the Democratic National Committee, and, separately, Guy Gabrielson, the chairman of the Republican National Committee; both men resigned. Such evenhandedness caused Peter Wyden of *Coronet* magazine to call Williams the 'politician without politics.' As Williams put it, 'A man that's going to be crooked is not going to be crooked just because he's a Republican or a Democrat.'

"In March 1949, Williams announced on the Senate floor, 'Mr. President, I have information that, if the books of the Commodity Credit Corporation were examined, we would find that over $350 million is unaccounted for.' The Secretary of Agriculture, Charles Brannan, publicly rebuked Williams, but it turned out that Williams was dead right. Eventually, 131 warehousemen who had converted millions of dollars' worth of grain to their own use were charged with criminal conversion or embezzlement.

WHAT DO YOU STAND FOR?

"When the Internal Revenue Service informed Williams that he had been delinquent in paying his income taxes, he investigated and discovered that not only had he properly paid his taxes, but an IRS employee had juggled taxpayer accounts (Williams among them) and embezzled $30,000. Williams kept asking questions, and eventually 125 IRS employees were convicted and 388 were fired or quit, including the top five IRS officials. *Look* magazine called Williams 'the taxpayer's unofficial prosecutor.' Williams, according to the magazine, 'single-handedly has unearthed so many administration scandals that thousands of taxpayers have come to regard him as their personal ambassador.'

"Williams was one of the first to raise questions about suspicious ties between Sherman Adams, President Eisenhower's closest advisor, and Bernard Goldfine, a wealthy Boston industrialist. Adams later resigned. Years later, in the 1960s, Williams exposed the criminal exploits of Bobby Baker, the powerful secretary of the Senate Democrats and Lyndon Johnson's protégé. Baker had amassed a personal fortune of $2.1 million by the age of thirty-four on an annual salary of $19,600. Johnson's close association with Baker never became a significant political issue for the President, but in 1964 LBJ was terribly agitated about Williams's pursuit of the Baker matter. We now know from Michael Beschloss' 1997 book *Taking Charge* and its transcripts of the Johnson White House tapes that at one point Johnson got Senate Majority Leader Mike Mansfield to shut down the Senate's investigation of Baker. Johnson also said to Mansfield on May 14, 1964, 'We'll just have to go after Mr. Williams…He's a mean, vicious man.' Whether Johnson actually followed through is unknown, but as John Barron reported in *Reader's Digest* back in 1965, the heat directed at Williams was enormous.

"Baker and his cronies tried to 'silence Williams' sources, to deceive him with false leads, to smear his character, even involve his family.' Strangers from Washington began showing up in tiny Millsboro, Delaware, asking questions about Williams. The IRS summoned the Senator to explain his 1963 tax return, which of course had been properly computed and filed. *The Washington Evening Star* reported that Williams' mail was even intercepted. 'The Senate should be totally outraged,' the newspaper said in an editorial. 'Obviously, someone high in the Executive branch issued the instructions for this monitoring. Nothing of the sort, as far as anyone knows, has ever been done before.'

"'I have plenty of time…and I am not about to be intimidated,' the beleaguered Williams, sounding a bit like Jimmy Stewart in *Mr. Smith Goes to Washington*, warned his colleagues. 'In fact, my curiosity and determination grow as resistance intensifies.' Eventually, Bobby Baker was convicted of theft, income-tax evasion and conspiracy.

"Williams was willing to stand up to any President, Republican or Democrat, and the most powerful corporate interests in his own backyard. Throughout his political career, he refused to accept political contributions but instead ran his campaigns through the state Republican Party. He had no campaign manager and no campaign organization. Today if a person of Williams' modest background expressed an interest in running for Congress, he or she would probably have trouble getting anyone in either party to listen.

"John Williams and Philip Hart could not have been more different from each other politically (a conservative Republican and a liberal Democrat), geographically (Delaware and Michigan), and professionally (the owner of a small business and a big-city lawyer). But both men were dead honest, modest and unpretentious.

"An infantryman wounded on D-Day during World War II, Hart had earlier earned a bachelor's degree at Georgetown University and a law degree at the University of Michigan. Before entering politics, he worked in a Detroit law firm. As a novice political candidate in 1950, biographer Michael O'Brien noted in *Philip Hart: The Conscience of the Senate*, Hart did not interact well with strangers, was reluctant to ask people to vote for him, and sometimes even apologized for running for office. Hart lost his first election, for Secretary of State, and following a stint as a U.S. Attorney, he was elected to statewide office as Michigan's lieutenant governor in 1954 and was re-elected in 1956. He was elected to the Senate in 1958 and served there until his death from cancer in 1976.

"Hart was known as an author and sponsor of important legislation in the areas of civil rights (he was a leader in the fight for the 1956 Voting Rights Act), antitrust enforcement, and consumer and environmental protection. But most unusual, then and today, Hart frequently took difficult, courageous stands on issues directly against his own political self-interest. In late 1968, for example, a staff aide on the Senate Antitrust and Monopoly Subcommittee, which Hart chaired, proposed that the subcommittee investigate the automobile industry. As recounted in O'Brien's book, Hart met the aide, Donald Randall, in the hallway:

"'Don, I understand you're recommending we go into investigation of the automobile business,' Hart observed.

"'Yes, sir,' said Randall.

"'Do you know that I'm running for re-election next year?'

"'Yes, sir.'

"'Do you know I'm from Michigan?'

"'Yes, sir.'

"'You know that the biggest business in my state is the auto industry, don't you?'

"'Yes, sir.'

"'And do you know that if I lose, you lose?'

"'Yes, sir.'

"'Do you still want to do it?' Hart asked.

"'Yes, sir,' Randall replied.

"'Well,' Hart said, 'go do it.'

"For more than a year, Hart's subcommittee held hearings on abuses in the automobile-repair business. Hundreds of angry car owners, frustrated mechanics, and auto-industry experts testified about the rampant incompetence and exploding costs in the multibillion-dollar business. The owner of an automobile-diagnostic center in Denver testified that tests on 5,000 cars in his shop revealed that only one of every 100 cars was being repaired properly.

"One of the outcomes of Hart's hearings was the 1970 Motor Vehicle Information and Cost Savings Act, which mandated fragility standards for assembling automobiles. *Motor Trend* magazine said, 'Senator Hart is a man of courage. To attack a problem as large and politically explosive as automobile repair, especially for a Senator from Michigan, the home of the auto industry, is no small undertaking.'

"Hart was also upset by monopolistic practices in the communications and newspaper industry, and he held hearings on the subject. He was one of the few dissenting voices against the Newspaper Preservation Act in 1970, which gave a special exemption to competing newspapers that merged their business operations and fixed their advertising rates. 'Swift congressional rescue of the publishers,' Hart observed, 'must make fascinating reading for the blacks who, until the 1964 Civil Rights Act, had waited decades for relief from court convictions for eating in certain restaurants and hotels.'

"Today a Senate office building is named after Hart, and inscribed in marble is the following: *'This building is dedicated by his colleagues to the memory of Philip A. Hart with affection, respect, and esteem. A man of incorruptible integrity and personal courage strengthened by inner grace and outer gentleness, he elevated politics to a level of purity that will forever be an example to every elected official. He advanced the cause of human justice, promoted the welfare of the common man, and improved the quality of life. His humility and ethics earned him his place as the conscience of the Senate.'"*

Mᴀʀɪᴏ Cᴜᴏᴍᴏ served as governor of New York for three terms, from 1983 to 1994. In both speech and action, he has championed for greater commitment beyond ourselves and remains an example to us all when it comes to civic virtue and the hard choices that must sometimes be made. He speaks with a passion and reason that is difficult to ignore: "In analyzing the issues, we need to remember there is a place for ideology, but it is not first place. First place goes to good sense, no matter what political badge it happens to be wearing at the moment. Sometimes that's common sense...other times it may mean uncommon sense. We need to get beyond the beguiling simplistics and sound bites, blow away the blue smoke, take down the political mirrors, and be willing to accept the truth when we find it."

Like most people, I have struggled with the process of trying to understand exactly who I am, what I want to be, and how I should behave, for most of my life.

At this point I've concluded the answers come in two major categories: my obligations and my options. My principal obligations are to help my large family every way I can, to live by the law, fulfill my civic duties, and avoid hurting other human beings. Among the options available to me are participation in public service and political activity and generally seeking to follow the prescription of the ancient Hebrews, *tikkun olam*, which is to help repair the universe. There's not a lot an ordinary individual can do that will make a significant difference, but just trying seems to me virtuous.

Taking a position on the death penalty as Governor was both a matter of obligation and an option. I have chosen to oppose capital punishment because I believe the death penalty is inconsistent with the idea of *tikkun olam*, as I interpret it.

It's clear the position on the death penalty hurt me politically. Exit polls showed it might have cost me as much as five percent in 1994, when I lost by four percent. But I won three times before that, despite it.

In the long run, I'd rather have lost the election than to bring death back to New York as an official New York State policy.

JUDITH MEISEL is a Holocaust survivor of the *Kovno* Ghetto in Lithuania and the *Stutthof* Concentration Camp in Poland. Her experiences during and after World War II inspired a life-long crusade against bigotry and racism.

After witnessing the race riots of 1963, Meisel has pursued and persevered in a campaign to speak out against racism and the need for greater tolerance in her community and around the country. Her response comes from a conversation and the powerful documentary – *Tak for Alt: Survival of a Human Spirit* by Laura Bialis, Broderick Fox and Sarah Levy.

1. I stand for Freedom and the pursuit of happiness.
2. I believe that we must respect the differences in other people.
3. We must learn about each other.

4. We must stamp out hate (hate stops you from living).

5. I find that apathy is the most difficult condition to deal with.

6. The statement, "What can I do? – I'm only one person" upsets me very much. One person can do a lot!

I was having dinner, listening to the news. After an African-American family by the name of Baker moved into an all white neighborhood called Folcroft, a mob of people turned out taunting them, screaming, yelling at them, throwing all kinds of debris. And I was devastated because here I was in Philadelphia, in the city of brotherly love and it was like *Kristallnacht* (night of broken glass) in 1938, November 9th when the world sat and looked at what was happening in Germany and nobody did anything about it!

So, I baked some cookies and I went to the Bakers. I was called, "white trash," you name it. But I felt that if their homes were not safe, my home was not safe. If their rights are trampled on, my Jewish rights are trampled on at the same time.

I was a Holocaust survivor, but I could not talk about it. I did not want to traumatize my children. But that incident with the Bakers, it made an incredible mark on me. I knew that I had to tell my story.

Racism, bigotry…it's still happening all over the world, and we have to constantly work at it to see that this does not happen here or anywhere. We cannot afford to say, "What can I do? – I'm only one person?" One person can do a lot!

What Do You Stand For?

MOST PEOPLE MAY NOT RECOGNIZE CARL MUSCARELLO by name but are probably familiar with his picture. He's the sailor kissing the nurse in Alfred Eisenstaedt's 1945 photograph on V-J Day in Times Square. However, Muscarello prefers to be described as, "an Italian-American kid from Brooklyn, New York who has been fortunate in that happiness in my life has come from my children, their children, my family and friends and my belief in God." his story reflects the importance of a good reputation in service to his community.

The answer that I give to this question at the risk of being plagiaristic is as follows:

1. Know what you are doing. Love what you are doing. Believe in what you are doing.
2. Failure is a detour, not a dead end.
3. I always tried my best, and my best got better.
4. You fail when you stop trying.
5. You don't have a chance if you don't take a chance.

I was born in New York City in 1926, the third of eight children. My father, Sebastian, and my mother, Maria Grazia, both emigrated from a small town in Sicily, Italy. I could not speak English until I was about five years old. I was fluent in the Italian language, specifically the Sicilian dialect.

When I became a New York City Policeman, and later a detective, due to this talent I was assigned to intercept conversations from telephone wiretaps and hidden listening devices. The conversations were all in the Sicilian dialect. At the time, organized crime was controlled by the Sicilian Mafia, so I was assigned to infiltrate the mob to make controlled buys of contraband. You should have seen the look on some of the wise guys' faces when my true identify was learned. As I appeared in Court to testify against them, one screamed, "How could you do this?" as I was Italian just like they were. Yes, I was Italian, but not like them, and neither was my father, or my brothers who did back breaking work in the construction industry to support their families.

My name, I got it from my father. It was all he had to give. It was now mine to use and cherish for as long as I may live. If I lost the watch he gave me, it could always be replaced, but a black mark on our name can never be erased. It was clean the day I took it, and a worthy name to bear when he got it from his father. There was no dishonor associated with it, so I made sure to guard it wisely.

After all is said and done, I was glad my name was spotless when I handed it to my son, Tony. True to form he has only enhanced it. And all my nephews have done the same.

JOE MOROS is a teacher at Bernice Ayer Middle School in San Clemente, California. When he faced the violence of hate first hand, Moros took direct action in his own classroom.

In 1993, one of my former students, Steve Woods, was speared through the brain with a sharpened paint roller in a tragic, hate-related killing linked to gang violence. Remembering this boy's smiling face from his entire sophomore year in my English class, I had a very hard time understanding this tragedy. In the ensuing weeks, I was further disheartened in seeing that the X-ray photography of his brain, with the paint roller protruding, was being used as a poster to fuel the passage of a racially-motivated law to bar educational and medical assistance to children of illegal immigrants in California.

Earlier that year, one of our high school students had been sentenced to ten years in jail for viciously beating a homosexual nearly to death. The media descended upon our school, as well as gay-rights protestors. I remember going to the principal after this incident and saying, "We ought to do something about this." He agreed, and he went back to his office, and I went back to my classroom. And we did nothing about it.

After Steve's death, I remembered my earlier words to the principal and decided that I had to do something to quell the hatred and violence that was threatening to engulf my school, city and the entire nation. I then wrote a grant to design and pilot Promoting Tolerance through Understanding, (www.teachtolerance.org), a high school elective class at our school.

In an effort to stop our local and national epidemic of hate and youth crime, this course addresses the issues of prejudice, hatred, discrimination, and the end result of these societal ills – the violence that often is the aftermath. There is no place for criticism, hostility, or ridicule in my classroom. I do my best to create an environment in which a student feels safe – safe to speak his or her views, safe to be him or herself, safe to learn. My classroom is a prejudice-free zone. We are now in the seventeenth semester of the Tolerance class, and I am happy to see many students interested in taking it. Many students mention that they feel that the campus is a much more peaceful place since its inception.

PAUL **W**ATSON is a Canadian conservationist and environmental activist who has become internationally renowned for his daring and direct approach to the field of wildlife conservation. As one of the founding members of the Greenpeace Foundation, Watson sailed into a nuclear test site in Alaska in 1971. In '75 he became the first man to place his body between a harpoon and a whale, capturing the attention of the media worldwide.

In 1977, Watson founded the Sea Shepherd Conservation Society. Under his leadership, the society has been in the forefront of marine wildlife conservation. Sea Shepherd's activities include bringing an end to pirate whaling in the North Atlantic by ramming the whaler *Sierra* off the coast of Portugal in 1979, and successfully documenting illegal whaling in Soviet Siberia after a six-hour pursuit by the Soviet Navy and Air Force in 1981, as well as interfering in the activities of sealing fleets off the eastern coast of Canada. Throughout it all, Watson remains steadfast in what he believes – that man needs to embrace a deeper concern and commitment to the other species of the world.

My personal code of ethics has been shaped by my childhood

activities in protecting wild animals, by my travels as a merchant seaman in my late teens and early twenties, and by my experience with the American Indian Movement in 1973 during the occupation of Wounded Knee.

I have devoted my life to wildlife and habitat conservation efforts. This began when as a child of nine I befriended a beaver. A year later, I discovered that my friend had been killed in a leg hold trap. I became very angry and began to hunt down trap-lines, freeing animals and destroying traps.

My travels from 1967 to 1974, primarily in Asia and Africa, made me realize that I had been born with privilege as a North American even if I was poor. I learned to never complain about lack of material comfort and to appreciate what I had.

In 1973, Wallace Black Elk taught me in Wounded Knee that to be a warrior I had to overcome any fear of death and that I should be unconcerned about what people thought of my actions so long as I believed that my actions were just. He taught me to be unconcerned about the strength of the opposition and to not worry about winning or losing. "You do what you do because it is the right thing to do, the just thing to do, and thus the only path to take."

In 1974, after blocking a Soviet harpoon, a wounded Sperm whale could have taken my life but instead of crushing me, very deliberately and painfully slipped beneath the surface of the water and died as we remained in eye to eye contact from only a few feet away. I vowed from that moment on to protect whales for the rest of my life.

My principles were tested recently when I led a campaign

to oppose the illegal killing of whales by the Makah Indian tribe of Washington State. The hunt is not legal under international law, and although I kept the focus on our reasons for opposing the hunt, I was accused of racism and denounced by people who were once my allies in the Native American Movement. I was told that being anti-whaling was anti-Indian and thus racist.

In my heart I knew that I was anti-whaling and this had nothing to do with the race of the whalers. I continued to stand guard for the whales because I knew that I was just and right in doing so, and accusations of racism were invalidated by the strength of my convictions and the knowledge that I had the support of Makah Elders and other Native Americans on my side.

My allegiance is to the Earth and all her species before it is to my own species. I believe in the continuum of life, and I know that decisions we make today will profoundly impact the nature of the world tomorrow. I am more concerned about what people will think of my actions hundreds of years from now than I am about the opinions of people who share my generations in the present.

GORDON YOUNGS has more than twenty-five years experience in employee relations and personnel management with both public agency and employee (labor union) perspectives. He has served on committees for the League of California Cities, and the National League of Cities, as well as the National Public Employer Labor Relations Association. Youngs currently serves as personnel director for the city of Brea, California. His story demonstrates what it means to play by the rules.

Professionally, my principles relate to my role as a public employee:

- Accountability for those things over which I have control.
- Loyalty to the organization, my supervisor, my co-workers, and my community.
- Honesty and fairness with regard to all the people affected.
- Consistency, which fosters trust.
- Leadership, by demonstration and inspiration.

Bureaucracy in many public organizations can have the effect of reducing personal accountability. In times of conflict, some people retreat to the "rule of law," rather than take responsibility for change, thereby demonstrating moral leadership. Loyalty to the organization, which is a commitment to purpose and service, is misperceived by the public, our client and employer, as defense of waste and abuse. It takes an insistence on honesty and fairness, consistency in effort and character, and leadership by example to create and maintain trust. Those are the principles I value, and I can only be effective if I can conduct myself accordingly.

The principles I apply to my job also apply to my personal life, but I am also influenced by what I have learned, things my father taught me, and things that have been reinforced many times over by people I respect – teachers, coaches, supervisors, friends:

- Be responsible to myself, and live up to my own expectations.
- Take care of those people and things dearest to me, and protect those who cannot protect themselves.
- Be able to look in the mirror and see someone I respect.

My friend and former supervisor called it "a combination of character and competency," and that is as close as I could ever come to describing it.

To illustrate what I mean, I have to go back to when I was a teenager, and how someone else inspired me.

I was just gaining some skills at golf, and I most enjoyed the days when friends and I just played for the love of the game. My father would drop us off at the course, and we would fashion a competition with each other, betting a nickel or dime a hole, just to make the game more fun. One day, my friends and I came to the seventh hole, a long par four which required a long second shot over a ravine.

My friend Roger and I were about equal in ability. The other two guys, Bob and Don, were a little better and a little worse, respectively. Roger drove the ball well off the tee, toward some small trees on the right. I hit an "okay" drive to the left side. Bob banged his drive deep down the middle, and Don sliced one just in play to the right, twenty yards or so behind Roger.

What Do You Stand For?

Don reached his ball first and got ready to hit. Roger moved down the fairway to his ball, and stepped back to the left to clear a path for Don. I watched from the left side of the fairway as Don tried to hit a hard three-wood to the green, and then as the ball ricocheted off a small tree and hit Roger hard in his ribcage.

Roger went down clutching his side and grimacing in pain. He was in tears when I got there, but trying to joke about it. "Just help me up," he told us. As he came to his feet, he looked at Don, who was obviously worried and apologized repeatedly.

"Did you try to bank one off me deliberately?" Roger said. He laughed, and Don looked relieved. When Roger went to his ball and prepared to hit, his swing was not as fluid as earlier that day. His follow-through was abrupt and his shot tumbled down to the ravine. The pain was clearly affecting him, but he grimaced and kept going, ending up taking a double-bogey on the hole.

When I finished my bogey, Roger came over and handed me a nickel. "What's this?" I asked. "Your winnings," he said with a forced smile. "I can't take this; you were injured. The bet was off," I insisted. "No," he said, "that was just 'rub of the green' and you won the hole. I would have collected if you missed a putt or hit one out of bounds. That's just the way the game is played."

No matter how much he hurt, he played by the rules. While I was intent on being courteous, as we are all taught to be, he was telling me it was consistent with the courtesy of the game to accept wins and losses gracefully, to acknowledge an opponent's good luck and disregard your own bad fortune. But, you say, it was only a nickel wager. No, it was more than that. It was setting the stage for the times when he and I had more on the line, when we would expect, even depend on each other, to do the right thing. I knew then what it meant to be loyal to my commitments, even if I had a good excuse for begging out. It was a moment of character, and I was the recipient of much more than a nickel's worth of insight.

ONE OF THE THINGS that distinguishes great sports figures from the rest of the pack is their direct and honest approach to both their work and their life. They consistently strive to live up to their own highest standards for both themselves and the rest of us. A good example is Joe Paterno, head football coach at Pennsylvania State University. His approach to the game and life is revealed in a couple of simple, yet challenging statements: "I have always had the ability to concentrate on what has to be done and not worry about things I can't do anything about. If I can do something about it, I go after it and try to get it done by giving my best shot. If I succeed, fine, but if I fail I put it behind me."

When college sports violations seem to be unremitting, Paterno's story reminds us that there *are* coaches who do play by the rules.

The principle I try to live by is to treat others as I would like to be treated; be honest and fair.

An example of a time when my principles were tested was during recruiting some years ago, I tried to recruit a kid out of Cincinnati who was a great, great football player. He would have made a great impact on the success of our football team. I went to his house, sat down and talked with him and his dad, trying to sell them on Penn State.

The dad said to me at the end of my conversation, "Yeah that's fine coach, but what are you going to do for the kid?" I asked him what he meant by that. I said I am going to give him whatever the NCAA grants him. The dad then told me his son couldn't go to Penn State unless he could get a few extra things. I told the father I couldn't do that. I wished him my best and walked away from him.

As much as we would have liked to have that young man be a part of our program, I stuck to my beliefs and followed the rules. The young man ended up enrolling at another institution, which I understand "took good care of him," and he went on to play professional football. But, I had not sacrificed my principles to get that young man to enroll at Penn State. Don't sacrifice your principles and beliefs to get what you want.

"Success without honor is like an unseasoned dish. It will satisfy your hunger, but it won't taste good."

IN HIS AUTOBIOGRAPHY, *NO FREE RIDE*, KWEISI MFUME remembers how difficult it was losing his mother to cancer. He quit high school and began working to support his three sisters. He also began hanging out on the streets, becoming a gang leader. Disillusioned with his lifestyle, the twenty-two-year-old made a decision to change his life. He earned a high school equivalency diploma, graduated *magna cum laude* from Morgan State University, and developed an interest in politics while working as a disc jockey.

During his seven years of service on the Baltimore City Council, Mfume led efforts to diversify city government, improve community safety, enhance minority business development, and divest city funds from the apartheid government of South Africa. In 1986, he was decisively elected to the Congressional seat that he would hold for the next ten years.

As President and Chief Executive Officer of the National Association for the Advancement of Colored People, Kweisi Mfume, whose West African name means, "conquering son of kings," continues to work in his community by helping youth recognize their own potential.

> Back in 1994, I had the occasion to speak with a young gang member who reminded me very much of myself about thirty years ago. Throughout the course of our conversation, I tried to get him to recognize the possibility of attending college, as opposed to a life centered on the street. In spite of the cajoling and derision of his friends, I could feel him wanting to believe me. As I walked away from him, our eyes met, and I saw the stare I had seen a hundred times before. I, too, have given it and received it. It's the stare of death secretly crying out for life, hoping against hope that someone will decipher it.
>
> After I left that street corner, a part of me stayed behind. I couldn't erase the faces I had just encountered and confronted. In one quick twist of a moment, life had played a cruel hoax on me. Because I never gave up on myself, I know

that I can never give up on these kids. They are not beyond rescue or redemption any more than they are beyond hope or help. They are a part of the other America, trapped and lost in every big city and every small town. They are the ones we pass by in our cars as we lock our doors. They are the ones who flirt with death and test our limits. They become teenage parents much too soon, and give up on life much too fast. No matter how much we would like to dismiss their existence, they are, and continue to be among us.

My principles and my inspiration lie inextricably bound together. My own faith, hope, courage, integrity, and hard work seek those qualities in other people, and in finding them, I am inspired. I am inspired a hundred times a day. That inspiration enables me to continue to reach out to that young man and attempt to pull him to this side of the widening crevasse – to pull every young man and woman across the chasm of hatred, poverty, ignorance and despair. And to see their eyes finally open in recognition, hope, and joy would be the ultimate reward of that inspiration and principle – of all my life's work.

MATT SANCHEZ left Santa Barbara only twice – once when he joined the Marines, the other, when he went to prison.

In 1987, as the leader of the Eastside Hoods, Sanchez called the heads of the area's other twelve gangs together. After several shootings, he wanted to put an end to the violence. The peace treaty lasted for five years. In 1992 after the stabbing of a rival gang member, he called everyone together once again. This time the kids ended the negotiations with a touch-football game and a barbeque. That activity led to a bus trip to the mountains. Dubbed "Hoods in the Woods," the program allowed gang members to stop "banging" and start working together and trusting one another.

After the deaths of several friends including his own brother, and a prison term, Sanchez finally realized that the only way to stem the violent behavior was to expand his program into one that would support and encourage gang members to put aside the past and embrace the future of possibilities, a future that would not only end the gang activity but allow kids to be the best they were meant to be.

Ten years later, Sanchez's vision of rival gang members and "at-risk" kids learning teamwork, trust and responsibility has emerged as a positive force. With a dramatic and documented fifty-five percent reduction of gang-related activity in the greater Santa Barbara area, All For One currently manages a membership of over two hundred youth and thirty mentors. "The purpose," he says, is "helping kids lead more productive lives; to see the end of the road before they reach the end of the road."

Like Kweisi Mfume, Sanchez shows his commitment in helping "at-risk" kids see beyond themselves to a greater responsibility to their families and each other.

One thing about All For One is that we're on-call 24-hours a day. We've gotten calls at one in the morning, three in the morning, from kids who found themselves in predicaments that they don't want to be in and need a way out.

One time, this kid got stabbed, and his friends called up and said, "It's getting crazy over here. Can you come over?" Rival gang members were hanging around saying that it was the dead kid's fault, which is a slap in the face to the kid's friends. Words went back and forth. So I went down there.

It was about twenty kids to eight, and it was confrontational. But the eight from the rival gang were older, so they had more of a fearless attitude. Normally, these kids wouldn't dare attack me because of my status as a former gang leader, but all that went out the window.

I pulled the older ones to the side. I'm trying to tell them that I know how they feel. "Look," I said, "you gotta understand where these youngsters are coming from." But they didn't really want to hear me. They were saying that they lost a friend also because he was now in prison.

Then I spoke to my youngsters – these are the ones that we've been working with and I said, "Look, this is the time, right here. This is where everything that we've done in the program, this is where it counts, right here. You can let this guy over here talk his talk, but if you're going to fall into that, then take a good look around and think about whose funeral you'll be going to next. You better tell everybody, right now, how much you love 'em because you're not going to see them again. Now, if you really love them, you wouldn't think of yourself right now. You'd think of him, then you'd think about his parents and everybody else because that's who's going to be left. Right now, you're thinking about yourself. You're thinking 'I don't care. I'm going to do this and if I die, I die.' That's fine. You don't care. You look at that as a man but that's not really how a man looks at things."

They knew that we've been telling them this through our time together. We tell them stories about the friends that we've lost; stories about prison, all the stuff that nobody talks about. I look at these kids and I don't want them to go through the same thing I went through. They bought into a lie, and I bought into the same lie: that that's the life, being a gang member. "This is what you're going for right now! This is the price you're going to pay, right here!"

And so they knew. They knew that when I tell them, or when some of our mentors talk to these kids, they could see it in our eyes; they could hear it in our voices, that what we're telling them is true. They know that we've lived it; that we're still living through it.

Just then, the older kids began challenging the younger crowd. "Come on! Come on!" The younger ones' looked at each other until one said, "You know what? Leave it. Just leave it. Let him go." And they walked away. And I was proud of them.

For his selfless commitment to "at-risk" youth, Matt Sanchez has been honored with a Certificate of Commendation from the State of California, 2000; The California Wellness Foundation's California Peace Prize, 2000; and Santa Barbara County Probation Department's 1999 Distinguished Service Award.

DALE DYE speaks the language of the Marine Captain he once

was – direct, no-nonsense, unequivocal. Perhaps this is one reason why his company, Warriors, Inc., is the top media military advisor, responsible for the technical accuracy and training on such films as *Platoon*, and *Saving Private Ryan*, as well as the HBO series, *Band of Brothers*. For Dale Dye, the word *sacrifice* has a special, unalterable meaning.

On March 14, 1968, I killed a man. No doubt about it. This wasn't one of those shoot at muzzle-flash or fleeting-shadow-in-the-jungle deals. This was homicide at a range of about fifteen meters. The weapon was an M-16 rifle, and I clearly saw the whites of my victim's eyes through the rear sight aperture as I squeezed the trigger. I put three rounds into his upper body and he dropped like a wet sandbag.

As everyone still upright in Echo Company, 2nd Battalion, Third Marines on that day was engaged in a brutal running firefight with equally desperate soldiers from the North Vietnamese Army's 324 C Infantry Regiment, there was neither time nor inclination to contemplate morality or ethical questions.

I don't know if I killed anyone else that day, but the one carrying the RPG (rocket) rounds was confirmed. We dug in on a spit of sand and scrub pine when night came, expecting a counter-attack from the NVA (North Vietnamese Army) survivors who were trapped by our attack with their backs to the South China Sea. My watch that night was scheduled for the final two hours before dawn, so I was among the lucky survivors who was allowed to curl up in the bottom of my hole for an hour or two wrapped in a poncho-liner. Exhausted, shocked, and numb, sleep would not come. The image of the man I killed would not leave my mind. I saw his face on the back of my eyelids. What I had – on that miserable night in the northern provinces of South Vietnam – was an ethical crisis of monumental proportions.

My Sunday school upbringing was in mortal conflict with my rational view of soldierly conduct and survival instinct. Like it or not – and I sure as hell didn't at the time – I had become a murderer at age twenty-two. And if the good folks who taught me right from wrong from a religious perspective had it right at all, I was doomed from that moment for all eternity. I shivered and shook and wondered if what God had in store for me could be worse than Vietnam.

I crawled from my hole and made my way through the dark to the Company Command Post. Maybe I could relieve somebody there of his radio watch. Maybe I'd get killed and relieved of the burden I was feeling. I didn't know for sure, but our Company Gunny was on watch when I slid into the CP and mumbled something about not being able to sleep anyway.

"What's on your mind, Dye?" He just stared, noting how my hand shook when I reached for the radio to receive a SitRep (Situation Report) from one of the Listening Posts outside our perimeter.

"Nothin', Gunny. Just feelin' a little weird, is all."

"Blew one away today, didn't you?" Gunny knew everything that happened in Echo Company and he knew his Marines.

"I don't know if I can do this shit."

It was the damndest thing. Gunny – the kick-your-ass, kill-em-and-eat-em, spitting image of John Wayne – reached out and touched my cheek. It was just a touch and the hint of white teeth in the dark, but it was all I needed to start blubbering. He held onto me and whispered things about his own experience in the frozen Chosin Reservoir in Korea. He'd killed a bunch of Chinese in a hill fight one night and had the same reaction. He understood and wanted to let me know he understood.

We stood watch together that night, answering routine calls on the radio, watching for movement to our front and flanks – becoming professional fighting men together with the tacit understanding that what we had chosen to do required a great leap of faith beyond what most mortals will ever be required to make.

Just before dawn, the Gunny dragged me from the CP and walked with me over to the area where our KIA's (killed in action) had been wrapped in ponchos and tagged for evacuation. He knelt by one of the corpses and exposed the face of a Marine I knew well. "It ain't about you, Dye. It's about him…and all the other Marines in this outfit and all the other outfits. You fight and, when the time comes, you kill to prevent this. If that's murder…if that's a sin…then there ain't no justice. I couldn't live with that thought in Korea, and you ain't gonna be able to live with it in the Nam. It's a hard-assed, horrible thing we gotta do, son, but better we do it than people who can't handle it.

You gotta understand," the Gunny told me as we stood to face the dawn, "there are things in this life a whole lot bigger and more important than you and me. We got just one life to give, and if we give it to support or defend others, then we done good. God knows that and we should too."

I learned a lot that day, but it was not in the nature of an epiphany. It took years for some of the lessons to become part of what I stand for today –

- Take counsel of your fears but don't be afraid to wrestle with moral questions. The internal dispute, once resolved, will frequently put you on solid ground when the next tough question arises.
- Understand and appreciate the sacrifices of others. It gives you a sense of pride, belonging and unity.
- Back off from your own concerns and bear in mind that there is usually something larger, and more important, than yourself.
- Stand for your fellow man. He's generally worth it.
- Ponder the soldier when times are tight and understand that he's the ultimate and noblest of all public servants. If he's willing to die for you, be worth that sacrifice.

Thanks Gunny

11

a selfless spirit

ALTHOUGH FAITH IS NOT AN ETHICAL VALUE, its importance in driving ethical conduct should not be underestimated. In fact, the word faith comes from the Latin *fidere* meaning 'to trust.' According to the Dictionary of Philosophy and Religion, "Faith is an attitude or belief which goes beyond the available evidence."

Trusting can sometimes be difficult, but it can uplift and strengthen our resolve to reach beyond ourselves and become caring and compassionate of others.

Compassion – seeing ourselves in another – is at the heart of the ethical value of Caring. The German philosopher Arthur Schopenhauer said, "Compassion is the basis of morality." It's reflected in kindness, giving, and a genuine concern for others. It's acting "outside ourselves," as Dale Dye reminds us.

But it all comes back to placing our confidence, our trust, in a person or thing.

"Faith," Saint Augustine said, "is to believe what you do not see; the reward of this faith is to *see* what you believe."

DURING HIS THIRTY-FIVE-YEAR CAREER in the Marine Corps, General Charles Krulak served two tours of duty in Vietnam and rose through several command and staff positions to become Commandant of the Marine Corps and a member of the Joint Chiefs of Staff.

At a Joint Services Conference on Professional Ethics in January 2000, General Krulak opened the meeting with the following stated goals – "We study and discuss ethical principles because it serves to strengthen and validate our own inner value system...it gives direction to what I call our moral compass. It is the understanding of ethics that becomes the foundation upon which we can deliberately commit to inviolate principles. It becomes the basis of what we are...of what we include in our character. Based on it, we commit to doing what is right. We expect such commitment from our leaders. But most importantly, we must demand it of ourselves."

His story not only underscores the role of faith, but demonstrates that the powerful moments in life can and do re-emerge to help clarify the principles we believe in and strive to live.

> In December 1965, while serving as a rifle company executive officer in Golf Company, 2nd Battalion, 1st Marines, I went ashore with my unit and one of my dearest friends, a second lieutenant that was serving as a platoon commander, in South Vietnam as part of Operation Harvest Moon. This second lieutenant was a quiet, gentle, but very strong leader, and he was a man of deep faith in God. I did not fully appreciate it at the time, but the events of that day changed the

course of my life. You see his example in the crucible of combat has inspired my own faith to this very day.

As my company of about one-hundred-fifty Marines was moving down a trail bordered on one side by very thick foliage and on the other by a wide open rice paddy, we were ambushed. My friend's platoon had been the lead element in our formation. The enemy initiated the ambush with a large caliber weapon, hitting my friend twice, shearing off his leg and tearing through his chest. I was wounded at nearly the same time, but my wounds were not nearly as severe as his. As I crawled to his position, he quickly asked if I was okay. After I responded that I was fine, he immediately asked about the condition of his Marines. When I told him that they too were fine, he looked to the sky and thanked God repeatedly until he lost consciousness. I was amazed by his selfless spirit and his tremendous faith in the Lord. Still, for the next eleven years, while never forgetting his courage and faith, I failed to follow his example. And despite having a beautiful family, a thriving career, and a life rich with tremendous blessings, I was profoundly unhappy.

In 1976, while assigned to the U.S. Army's Command and General Staff College, that all changed when I met an Army Chaplain in the body of a Chicago Bears linebacker. This gentleman was a Vietnam War hero, a West Point sports star, and a first-class, tough soldier. He immediately recognized my unhappiness and would not accept any of my sorry excuses for what was causing it.

Through his persistence and example, as well as my

memory of my dear friend in Operation Harvest Moon in December 1965, I found the courage to put God first in my life, to pledge myself to His service. Despite the trials and challenges of the last twenty-three years, I have never wavered from that promise. My faith now anchors my entire perspective, strengthening the lessons of right and wrong that I learned as a child; giving far greater meaning to my daily actions, decisions, and example; helping me to order my priorities; and filling me with the joy of God's love and salvation. My faith reinforces – and is reinforced by – the core values of the institution to which I have dedicated my professional life, the United States Marine Corps.

The Marine Corps' core values – Honor, Courage, and Commitment – are the defining qualities of a Marine. They are mutually reinforcing and dependent. If one quality is strong, it supports the others; if one is weak, the others suffer. Honor is a well-developed sense of right and wrong. We boil it down to the simple expression that "Marines do not lie, cheat, or steal. Marines treat all people with dignity and respect."

Courage, particularly moral courage, is the willingness to do the right thing, no matter the personal cost or sacrifice. It is the foundation and source of physical courage, which is more often associated with military heroism. Finally, Commitment is selfless devotion to our faith, the Marine Corps, our fellow Marines, and our family and friends. Easy to remember, more challenging to live by, these are the standards to which all Marines are held.

In this day and age, as we are constantly challenged

by attacks on our sensibilities and our values, I am still heartened by the example of my fellow lieutenant and dear friend in Vietnam. He embodied the Christian faith and the Marine Corps' core values, which I measure myself against. His willingness to put himself at risk by leading from the front, his courage in the face of fire, his selfless concern for others despite his own injuries, and his determination to witness for God through his personal conduct represent the tremendous potential in all of us, as well as our greatest responsibilities. All around us, there are countless opportunities to serve the Lord and one another, to stand up for right in the face of daunting evil and injustice. It takes courage, sacrifice, and strength to do so, but we all have the responsibility to act, to get involved, and to demonstrate our faith for those who are looking for God's inspiration and may only find it through *our* example.

FOR HER COMMITMENT TO EDUCATION and community service, Celia Kerr has received the Youth of the Year and the Daughters of the American Revolution Good Citizenship awards. A *summa cum laude* graduate and Valedictorian of Hampton University's Honors College, Kerr enrolled in a PhD program in clinical psychology at the University of Missouri, St. Louis. Her story teaches us that with faith adversity can become a fuel instead of a distraction.

When we are children, our parents instill in us their principles and values that have guided them through the hills and valleys of life. Among the many lessons they teach are respect for self and others, independence, and the importance of compassion. As each child grows and learns about life, she takes the principles of her parents and forms them into principles of her own. Of the many lessons my mother instilled in me, the one that has led me throughout my path of success is keeping God first and all other things will fall into place. Resting on my mother's philosophy, I have created my own – keep God first and balance family and education second.

Fortunately, I have been blessed to be able to balance my dedication to family and education. I have been a good, responsible daughter, while keeping education a top priority. I participate in extracurricular activities, honor societies, academic clubs, and service organizations, while maintaining academic excellence. In all of this, I remain a faithful, obedient, and self-sufficient daughter to my mother. Thus far, keeping God first in my life has insured a successful collegiate career and a wonderful family life. However, there are times when God does place things in our lives to make us stronger. We may see those things as obstacles, but they really are tests of faith and endurance.

Recently, God gave me the ultimate test of faith – the threat of losing the most important person in my life. On January 4, 2001, my mother was diagnosed with a rare form of lymph nodal cancer. Since I am the only child of a single parent, caring for my mother falls on my shoulders. For the first time, I can no longer equally balance both family and education. I always imagined that my hardest decision in life would come in adulthood. Never did I think that my hardest would be to choose between my mother and my degree, more specifically, my future.

I firmly believe that education is the key to success. Without it, I cannot fulfill my hopes and dreams. Likewise, without the support and love of my mother, I would not have been able to get to this point of graduating into adulthood. I owe her my life and all that I have accomplished. I need both my education and my mother to continue living life. I am determined not to give up on either.

In this short month since my mother's diagnosis, I have grown in tremendous ways. Everyday is a struggle to continue this last leg of my journey of undergraduate education. I have dedicated weekends to completing the six-hour drive home for her chemotherapy treatments. I nurse her and care for her, as she has done for me. As she grows weaker, I see her spirit growing stronger. Instead of growing weary at the sight of her weaknesses and giving up on my education, I have chosen to use her strength as my driving force to complete my last semester at Hampton University in the top of my class.

After earning a master's degree, Kerr has taken a leave of absence from school to spend time at home. Although her mother has overcome lymph nodal cancer, she has recently been diagnosed with breast cancer. "We are very blessed to be together," she said, "and are holding strong to our faith and are determined to win our race again."

In a 1998 commencement address delivered at Loyola Marymount University in Los Angeles, Comcast Chairman Michael Armstrong answers the question with this story about caring.

Back in 1981, my wife and I were raising our three daughters in a comfortable little town in Connecticut. The community was all white, mostly WASP, and relatively affluent and seemed to have a quiet understanding to stay that way. But a minister neighbor of ours believed our town should share its school system and our community by bringing six to seven underprivileged, urban minority students to live and learn among us in a program called A Better Chance.

I'm sorry to say that the opposition was instant and powerful. Neighbors and friends, realtors and residents were against it. In fact, the opposition even filed lawsuits. But it was the right thing to do. And because a small group of us decided to stand for something, today scores of minority students are being given a better chance in that Connecticut town, and all have gone on to colleges and universities across the country. It was nothing heroic. But it enriched our lives.

I met Paul Newman when he called one afternoon to congratulate me about the release of my book, *The Lone Ranger's Code of the West.* He was quick to point out, though, that he did *not* make salad dressing nor had he worked with Robert Redford. "My name," he stressed, "is Paul S. Newman."

What Do You Stand For?

Newman was a comic-book writer so prolific that he was listed in the *Guinness Book of Records* with more than three-hundred-fifty comic-book titles to his credit. Beginning in 1947, he wrote more than 4,100 stories totaling about 36,000 pages – the equivalent of 120 mystery novels! Sadly, Paul Newman died not long after submitting his response about an event that took place early in his career.

As an Aristotelian, I believe that character is action.

Perhaps, my actions are best encapsulated in the admonition of an ancient Hebrew sage who urged one to *"Act justly, love mercy and walk humbly with thy God."* Though on further examination, while I strongly seek to act justly, I am not too merciful in discovering faults in others.

Years ago, I was sitting at a bullfight in Malaga. Despite the bull breaking a horn against the barricade, they let the fight continue. The crowd booed and many tossed their seat pillows into the arena. A Civil Guard, with his imposing black cockade hat, grabbed up a man one row behind me for throwing a pillow. Hundreds of pillows covered the arena floor, but he was the only person the police had started to arrest. And he was the only Black in the audience.

He was an American serviceman who, under Franco's rule, could not appear in public in uniform. The reason he was pulled from his seat was obvious – he was a Black sitting with a companion who was a white woman. As the Civil Guard started to lead him off, I left my wife and children, bounded up the stairs and began protesting. In rapid, ungrammatical Spanish, I shouted that the Civil Guard had no right to arrest this man unless they arrested some of the others who also had thrown pillows into the ring but happened to be white. The black soldier told me to walk away or I might get into trouble. I was too furious to care. I flashed my American passport, which in those days indicated one's profession. Mine was listed as "journalist," because I was then writing two, world syndicated newspaper comic strips, *The Lone Ranger* and *Laugh-In.*

I told the officer that if he didn't release the soldier, over two-hundred papers around the world would write up this incident, and I didn't think the then ruling Franco would be too pleased. The Civil Guard released the GI. When the soldier asked how he could thank me, I said, "Remember this. Some day I might need your help. I'm also a member of a minority. I'm Jewish."

PETER WESTBROOK is an Olympic medal-winning fencer who sees an inextricable connection between being your best and being compassionate. Although his principle and story are straightforward, his journey through anger and pain to compassion is a remarkable example for all of us to strive to demonstrate.

I stand foremost for serving the Creator. I stand for being the best that I can be. This can only be done by ridding yourself of old scars, wounds or idiosyncratic ways that stand in the way of serving the Creator, yourself, and others. My basic premise operates from this mold as much as possible.

When my mother was beaten and killed on a New Jersey bus for no reason, it allowed me to stand up for my convictions. I prayed to the Creator that the person who killed my mother would learn to appreciate other people's lives more and also her own. When the prosecutor's office wanted to put her away for many, many years, I disagreed in hope that if she could be remorseful, she could be used better on the outside serving humanity rather than in prison serving no one. I asked for her sentence to be shortened and it was.

What I also received from my mother's death is a completion of myself. I have a finer appreciation of sadness, loss, and compassion for others that one cannot understand unless it happens to him. However, most of the time the loss of a loved one through violence makes the person living experience so much anger, pain, and rage that it sometimes destroys them or stifles their growth, physically, mentally, emotionally and spiritually. It had the opposite effect on me. It made me more complete. God is good to me.

Peter teaches fencing, discipline, and much more, to inner city kids through the Peter Westbrook Foundation in New York City.

KIANGA MUNGAI'S GRANDMOTHER BIBI is an inspiration. Bibi's story demonstrates that people don't have a single moral strand as it extends from caring for others to caring for herself and her goals. Mungai's response comes from the John Templeton Foundation's Laws of Life essay contest.

Character qualities are what make people exceptional. One extraordinary person whom I really admire is my grandmother. I call her "Bibi," which means "grandmother" in the Swahili language. Bibi's life has been quite inspirational to me, and she has three qualities that make her special. My grandmother has always shown compassion towards everyone she meets. She is a person with ambition. Bibi sets goals for herself and stays committed to achieving those goals.

What compassion she showed when her mother died. She willingly gave up her schooling and her youth to help her father rear her younger sisters and brothers. Cooking and washing clothes for the family, keeping the house clean, and checking her siblings' homework became part of her daily routine although she was still a young girl. My grandmother never complained or felt that life was treating her unkindly. She focused on making sure that the "little ones" were well cared for, and she tried hard to be a good role model for them. Through it all, she never lost her sense of ambition.

She loved education and dreamed of becoming a teacher. When she left school to help her father rear the younger children, she had completed only eighth grade. After years of caring for her young siblings, she enrolled in evening classes. In 1944, my grandmother graduated from the Philadelphia Standard Evening High School. She was thirty years old. Economic pressures kept her from going any further with her education at the time, but she was determined not to forget her dream.

Bibi went to work as a seamstress at a factory, and on the weekends she did domestic work for other people. She saved for some college courses. Finally, at age forty-eight, to the surprise of many friends and co-workers, she enrolled at Cheyney State College to study elementary education. When she told her employer that she was resigning in order to go to college, he laughed and said: "You're going to leave this job to go study? I'm paying you good money here! Do you think you can be a teacher? My daughter's a teacher. How can you be a teacher like my daughter?"

My grandmother did not let these disparaging remarks discourage her. Four years later, she graduated with a Bachelor of Science degree and began teaching in the Philadelphia Public School System. She remained for seventeen years.

When my grandmother retired after teaching, a scholarship was given in her name to a graduate of Overbrook High School. My grandmother was quite touched by this gesture and decided that she would continue the scholarship fund herself the next year. And she continued it the next year and the next. For twenty years, Bibi single-handedly funded a scholarship for a needy graduate of her neighborhood high school.

Some years ago she took a ceramics class. All the proceeds from the ceramic works that she made and sold were dedicated to her scholarship fund. She did this quietly and without a lot of fuss. Last year, my mother and a few of my grandmother's friends joined her to incorporate the Elvira

B. Pierce Scholarship Fund and registered it as a charitable organization. They held a big fund-raising luncheon and were able to give two larger scholarships in June 2000. They are planning a fundraiser this year also.

Although my grandmother is eighty-seven-years-old, she is still committed to helping needy students at Overbrook because she is a strong supporter of public education and neighborhood schools. Remembering how her dream of higher education was deferred for so long, she says, "I want to help more of our young people accomplish their dreams sooner."

Because of her ambition, compassion, and commitment my grandmother is an inspiration to me. When I listen to Bibi talk about her life, I am reminded of a patchwork quilt – bits and pieces of old cloth sewn into a masterpiece. Her compassion reminds me to think of others. Bibi's ambition has taught me to strive high in life and never to limit myself. My grandmother's commitment lets me know that I can do anything as long as I stay focused. Not only is my grandmother an inspiration in my life, but also in the lives of the many young people that she has helped to continue their education plans. Hopefully the tradition will continue, and I will possess character traits that my future grandchildren will admire.

JOHN TIMPANE is the Commentary Page editor for the *Philadelphia Inquirer*. He came to this position after more than twenty years as a teacher of college English at Lafayette College, Rutgers

University, and Stanford University, where he received a PhD in English and Humanities. Timpane has written opinion and perspective pieces for magazines and newspapers for more than thirty years. But his passion is poetry. His latest books include *It Could Be Verse* and *Poetry for Dummies*.

At one point a scribe challenges Christ to tell him "which commandment is the first of all." Christ responds by saying, "You shall love the Lord your God with all your heart and with all your soul and with all your mind and with all your strength" and "You shall love your neighbor as yourself."

I hesitate to say I love God, but I do feel immense wonder, curiosity, gratitude, reverence, and awe before creation. I "stand for" that because those convictions drive my reasons for doing things. If we value the creation around us, we will try to act as though we deserve to be here. I'm never sure I do deserve it, but I try to act as though deserving life is at least possible. That means acting with dignity, humility, compassion, openness, and readiness for correction and change.

Loving others as oneself drives to the heart of what I really stand for. We can't stand alone, and we can't pretend selfishness is everything. I do really believe that sacrifice is a good thing. The few really fine things I've done were those that broke out of my own concerns and helped somebody else. I try to act as if we all really are brothers and sisters. It doesn't always work, but it has enriched this life.

Where has another inspired me? Well, once I lost my job in brutal and unfair circumstances, and I had to walk down the street and tell my wife, whom I knew was as happy as she had ever been in life. I knew what my words would do to that happiness.

But when I told her the news, she responded with such instantaneous, heartfelt, unselfconscious grief that I realized – for the first time, and we had been married four years by then – that she genuinely did take my part, that for her, hearing something bad had happened to me hurt her down to the core. "You work so hard!" she cried. She really did love me, which meant bearing the emotional brunt of hardship. So even though I was suffering, I saw it was even worse for her because she loved me. I can say that from that moment on, whenever I have suffered, I've done so knowing others suffer worse. I regard my wife as a very good person with wonderfully intuitive powers of empathy and devotion, things I dearly wish I could achieve. And I try. My sincerest wish is to learn to love as my wife does.

BRADLEY JAMES is a composer, pianist, singer, and public speaker. He is the Founder and President of Only Little Things Music, Inc. which produced and distributes his recording "Gift of Love, Music to the Words and Prayers of Mother Teresa." It is the only recording Mother Teresa authorized to her words and prayers. He met Mother Teresa in 1987 and continued their relationship through a series of letters and visits. James' response reflects the influence of caring Mother Teresa had on him.

The name of my music company, Only Little Things Music, and the subject of the first song on my CD, "Gift of Love, Music to the Words and Prayers of Mother Teresa" come from something that Mother Teresa said to me frequently during the years I knew her. It is a phrase that she shared with many over the years, as if to stress its importance. Mother often said, "We are not called to do great things, only little things with great love."

During Mother's last trip to the United States, she was staying with her Sisters, The Missionaries of Charity Contemplatives in the South Bronx. It was a beautiful, clear, sunny day in late spring. Mother was in the convent sick in bed, spending time with the Sisters and receiving few visitors. The doorbell rang constantly when Mother visited, but this day it was unusually quiet. I was sitting in the parlor talking with two Sisters when the doorbell rang. They asked me to answer the door, as they were on their way into the convent. At the door was a smiling young teacher and her class of eighteen or twenty kindergartners who had come to see Mother and to bring her an enormous cake.

I called for the Sisters who came out, and they told the teacher that Mother was ill and not receiving any visitors. The teacher was very kind and understanding and handed the cake to the Sisters. The sweet faces of these little children in the sunny street drew several of the Sisters out of the house until here was a small crowd talking to the teacher and to each of the children. In all of the activity, I noticed one little boy, smaller than the rest, who was standing alone, looking a little sad. He was probably not the most popular kid in class, as no one seemed to notice him. I went over and started talking to him.

His sweetness and simplicity moved me very deeply. He never smiled. He told me that they were there to bring a cake to Mother "Teesa" because she was sick. He told me a few other things that were important to a little boy growing up in one of the poorest sections of New York. I asked his name and he asked me for mine.

All little boys like to have a few coins in their pocket, so as they were gathering on the sidewalk to go back to school, I reached into my pocket and put all my pocket change into his dirty little hand. His eyes lit up as he put the coins into his pocket. The teacher began to line the kids up while we stood back and watched these adorable little children march back down the street. We couldn't take our eyes off of them. Suddenly, the little guy I had been talking to broke ranks and ran back to me. He threw his arms around my leg and said, "Thank you, Mister. Nobody ever talks to me." He took out a nickel and said, "Give this to Mother 'Teesa,' and tell her the rest is for my mom." Then, he ran back to join his class, smiling.

He didn't have a lot to give, but the little he had, he gave with great love. By the way, his name was Angel.

HOWARD **C. C**UTLER, **M.D.**, is an author and psychiatrist based in Phoenix, Arizona. Co-author with H.H. the Dalai Lama of the highly acclaimed international bestseller, *The Art of Happiness: A Handbook for Living,* Dr. Cutler lectures and offers workshops on happiness (theartofhappiness.com) throughout the United States. Dr. Cutler is currently collaborating with the Dalai Lama on the third volume in *The Art of Happiness* series.

I've come to the firm conviction that there is little else in life that is as important and worthwhile as the deliberate cultivation of kindness and compassion.

The Dalai Lama, a longtime friend who has been a source of great inspiration for me, is sometimes asked to boil his philosophy down to a single fundamental principle. To this difficult question, he often replies, "If you can, serve others. If not, at least refrain from harming them." As the years pass, I have become increasingly convinced that this simple principle, echoed throughout the centuries among many different traditions, is the key to living an ethical life. It is based on a sound understanding of the critical importance of compassion in our daily lives, and a realization of the inextricable link between our own personal happiness and kindness towards others.

In reflecting on the course of my life, it seems that I've come to this conclusion rather slowly. Perhaps this is because by inclination and conditioning (via training in science, medicine, and psychiatry) I had always considered myself a rational person, drawn to qualities such as the human intellect and reason. From this perspective, extensive talk about compassion and kindness had seemed a bit too sentimental for my taste, 'warm and fuzzy' concepts that were pleasant to hear about, and even inspiring at times, but without great relevance to the scientific model of the mind and human behavior. I was wrong. Using the tool of human reason, I began to objectively investigate the concrete physical, emotional, and social benefits of kind and compassionate states of mind – ultimately discovering that these qualities are not luxuries, but in fact necessities in the establishment of deep and meaningful relationships with others, and even crucial to our survival as a species.

In my own case, I was not fortunate enough to have a sudden epiphany, a galvanizing or defining "moment of principle" that set me on a course toward a kinder, more compassionate way of life. Instead, I discovered that each day offers many small "moments of principle" that test us and help increase our capacity to act on the principles that we believe.

The other day, a friend and I were driving on a busy street and happened to notice a middle aged woman standing by her car at the side of the road. The raised hood made it clear that she was having car trouble. My friend and I were both feeling particularly exhausted, and as each of us still had a lot of things to do that afternoon, we drove on past the woman, assuring ourselves that on such a busy road surely someone must have already stopped to help her and she must be waiting for a tow truck. If not, surely someone else will stop.

After speeding past the woman, we began to discuss whether we should have stopped just to see if she needed any assistance. After a mile-long debate, we finally decided to turn around and drive back. As it turned out, the woman was indeed having car trouble and had been standing in the scorching Arizona sun for a long time as a steady stream of motorists passed her by. She was immensely grateful for our very small effort in letting her use my friend's cell phone to call her husband and a tow truck and waiting with her until things were under control.

As my friend and I later drove off, we both noticed that our earlier physical exhaustion had completely disappeared; we were filled with tremendous energy in fact, and we marveled at how much our mood had improved by the simple act of stopping to help someone – once again, reinforcing the idea of the critical link between personal happiness and helping others.

I believe that once we're on the lookout, life presents many similar opportunities. Even trivial everyday events can be used as exercises in strengthening our inner values – consciously refraining from reacting with anger to a surly salesclerk or rude motorist, for instance, and choosing instead to respond with patience and tolerance, based on a clear understanding of our commonality with the other person and awareness of the underlying unhappiness that may be the source of that person's behavior.

Of course, I found that the mere conviction about the prime importance of kindness and compassion doesn't always automatically result in acting in accordance with this belief. And living by these principles doesn't mean one is perfect and selfless, acting solely for the welfare of others at all times. Under the trying conditions of daily life, it is sometimes difficult to respond with kindness, tolerance and forgiveness. It takes a concerted effort. It takes practice, and in my own case, I still have far to go. But I believe that living an ethical life begins with reflection on the benefits and importance of human kindness, an honest examination of our motives in our everyday dealings with other people, and making a sincere effort to transform our underlying motivation to become one of simply being of help to others – or, if we can't do that, at least avoid doing harm.

I MET EVAN SCHULTZ on a driving trip to visit the Acoma Pueblo outside Albuquerque, New Mexico. While discussing my book project with Evan and his parents, Evan told me of an incident that took place his previous year as a sixth grader. I asked if he would write it up and submit it. When he asked why, I told him that there were probably thousands of kids who had, at one time or another, experienced a similar situation and that his story might be able to help them.

Being twelve, I have not fully defined my principles yet, but recently I have come upon a "moment of principle," where standing up for another person came to an honest and satisfying solution.

At my school, there is a kid from Russia who was ridiculed for being himself. He speaks with a Russian accent. His mother buys all of his clothes, so he comes to school dressed in collared shirts buttoned all the way up and colorful dress socks. He is also very smart and does not hesitate to share his knowledge. The poor kid was called names and singled out as a nerd. After a while, I was sick of the whole situation. I felt very strongly that I needed to help stop it. However, I did not have a voice and could not get the other kids to stop. I did not let this fact discourage me, and I took the problem to the authorities. I spent a long session in the school counselor's office explaining and breaking down the situation for the counselor.

I left feeling much better, knowing that something would be done, and done in a way that would stop anyone who was making fun of him.

Even though I felt much better, I still had one concern. Retaliation. Someone could lash back at me, despite the fact that the counselor had assured me that my visit would be confidential. It's an interesting phenomenon that people can find certain things out. And they did find out. However, I figured that I could take care of myself, and helping someone who needs help was worth the consequences.

Since this, I have not heard one bad word thrown at him. I have not had one bad word thrown at me, and the whole situation has been resolved. Trust the power of your words.

A few weeks after receiving his response, I received a follow-up letter from Evan's mother, Virginia Schultz, that revealed a few more details behind Evan's story.

Evan had a hard time summoning up compassion for his Russian classmate, giving the example that besides being arrogant and rude, he made, what Evan perceived as, inflammatory remarks during group discussions about the superiority of all things Russian, whether it be weapons technology or Olympic athletes.

Speaking up had little effect. Evan said that the consensus was that it was best not to be harassed; therefore, being invisible was the best plan. At home, we commented that this strategy sounded incredibly like the one the Jews had espoused for so many decades in Europe – *"endure, and this too, shall pass."* It so happened that we made this comment during the sixth-grade Holocaust unit, which included having survivors visit and speak directly to students. The contact that Evan had over lunch with one survivor had a *huge* impact. When his attempts to stop the harassments were unsuccessful, he made an appointment with the mid-school counselor.

As parents, our job at home was to figure out how to get Evan to develop empathy and compassion for this child while, at the same time, recognizing that harassment is wrong no matter who the target is. Moreover, we felt it was his *duty* to speak up about it. We reminded Evan more than once of our visit to Atlanta, during which we visited the Martin Luther King National Monument and read Dr. King's compelling words, "Injustice anywhere is a threat to justice everywhere."

A few weeks later, Evan received The Spirit of the Community Award. The award is presented to two boys and two girls who best exemplify a spirit of cooperation, fair play, and tolerance as well as a genuine sense of caring. What makes it particularly unique is that the recipients are nominated and chosen by their peers. In order to prevent the award from becoming a "popularity contest," students must include the reason for their nominations.

TENZIN GYATSO is the fourteenth Dalai Lama of Tibet. He is both head of state (in exile) and the spiritual leader of the Tibetan people. He is admired and esteemed worldwide as a man who has championed policies of nonviolence. His consistent compassionate nonviolence, even in the face of great aggression, led to his receiving the Nobel Prize for Peace in 1989. His response to my questionnaire is simple and compelling.

> From my Buddhist viewpoint the mind plays a very dominant role. Actions and events depend heavily on motivation. A real sense of appreciation of humanity, compassion, and love, are the key points. If we develop a good heart, then whether the field is science, agriculture, or politics, since motivation is so very important, the result will be more beneficial. With proper motivation these activities can help humanity; without it they go the other way. This is why compassionate thought is so very important for humankind. Although it is difficult to bring about the inner change that gives rise to it, it is absolutely worthwhile to try.

In a follow-up, I asked the Dalai Lama if he would be willing to submit a personal story of compassion as well as answer a few related questions: *"How do you reconcile your sense of compassion and love with your objective of achieving justice and freedom for Tibet?*

Do you ever get angry with those who express violence to the Tibetan people? And if so, how do you get back on track?"

Due to the Dalai Lama's many commitments and travel schedule, he asked his translator and assistant, (The Venerable) Lhakdor, to provide the following:

If we are to improve this world, then the main source of peace and harmony is the practice of compassion and love in the day-to-day life of individuals. The practice of compassion and love is neither a luxurious pursuit of those who have nothing else to worry about nor a sign of weakness. These are the qualities without which our whole existence would be threatened or in chaos.

His Holiness has studied, in depth, about the benefits of positive human emotions like compassion and loving-kindness and has personally practiced these qualities in his dealings with other sentient [conscious] beings. Even when he was a child he saved the lives of hundreds and thousands of animals that were on their way to the butcher. In India he advised people to refrain from doing those types of business that would harm the lives of other sentient beings like running ammunition factories or arms trade, etc.

Based on this, His Holiness has developed a genuine conviction in the effectiveness of these positive human qualities in solving human problems, be they individual or social. He is also encouraged by the tremendous amount of resilience shown by many Tibetans in Chinese prisons through the practice of compassion and non-hatred even to their oppressors. Despite harsh treatment and long years of suffering they managed to maintain inner tranquility

One prisoner came up with the statement, "My time in a Chinese prison proved to be the best time for my spiritual practice." Another monk from Namgyal Monastery was in a Chinese prison for seventeen years. When he managed to leave Tibet and come to India, he met with His Holiness. One day, he mentioned to His Holiness that while he was in prison he faced danger on several occasions. His Holiness assumed that his life was in danger. But [the monk] continued, "I was in danger of losing compassion towards the Chinese."

His Holiness has always advised people that the struggle for the Tibetan cause is a just struggle, and therefore we should adopt *only* just and nonviolent methods to achieve what we want. Also, for the long-term benefit of both the Chinese and the Tibetans, the Tibetan issue should be resolved through the spirit of harmony, reconciliation and nonviolence. Violence leads to counter-violence, and, therefore, through violence one cannot solve the problem for good. He tries to solve the problem through dialogue and not confrontation.

Wherever he goes, His Holiness's main focus is how to develop compassion in the hearts of individuals and harmony among various religions, nations and communities.

A few weeks later, I received a couple of booklets written by the Dalai Lama: *Compassion and the Individual* and *The Global Community and the Need for Universal Responsibility*. The first offers the Dalai Lama's guidance on anger and details how compassion can become a powerful antidote:

"We should begin by removing the greatest hindrances to compassion: anger and hatred. As we all know, these are extremely powerful emotions, and they can overwhelm our entire mind...This is because anger eclipses the best part of our brain: its rationality. So the energy of anger is almost always unreliable. It can cause an immense amount of destructive, unfortunate behavior. Moreover, if anger increases to the extreme, one becomes like a mad person, acting in ways that are as damaging to oneself as they are to others.

"It is possible, however, to develop an equally forceful but far more controlled energy with which to handle difficult situations. This controlled energy comes not only from a compassionate attitude, but also from reason and patience. These are the most powerful antidotes to anger. Unfortunately, many people misjudge these qualities as signs of weakness. I believe the opposite to be true: that they are the true signs of inner strength. Compassion is by nature gentle, peaceful, and soft, but it is very powerful. It is those who easily lose their patience who are insecure and unstable. Thus, to me, the arousal of anger is a direct sign of weakness.

"So, when a problem first arises, try to remain humble and maintain a sincere attitude and be concerned that the outcome is fair. Of course, others may try to take advantage of you, and if your remaining detached only encourages unjust aggression, adopt a strong stand. This, however, should be done with compassion, and if it is necessary to

WHAT DO YOU STAND FOR?

express your views and take strong countermeasures, do so without anger or ill intent. You should realize that even though your opponents appear to be harming you, in the end, their destructive activity will damage only themselves. In order to check your own selfish impulse to retaliate, you should recall your desire to practice compassion and assume responsibility for helping prevent the other person from suffering the consequences of his or her acts.

"Thus, because the measures you employ have been calmly chosen, they will be more effective, more accurate, and more forceful. Retaliation based on the blind energy of anger seldom hits the target.

"So anger and hatred are always harmful, and unless we train our minds and work to reduce their negative force, they will continue to disturb us and disrupt our attempts to develop a calm mind. Anger and hatred are our real enemies. These are the forces we most need to confront and defeat, not the temporary 'enemies' who appear intermittently throughout life.

"For a person who cherishes compassion and love, the practice of tolerance is essential, and for that, an enemy is indispensable. So we should feel grateful to our enemies, for it is they who can best help us develop a tranquil mind!"

—Tenzin Gyatso, the Fourteenth Dalai Lama

Much of the time we tend to think of compassion in terms of the extraordinary moments, events which seem removed from our daily perspective. The monk's story of compassion towards his Chinese jailers is one example. However, a recent experience changed my thinking.

My neighbor, Sue Adams, is funny, wise and wonderful. Gifted with a sincere desire to help others, Sue has not only worked with community leaders and philanthropists to get the means and the methods implemented for a newly renovated homeless center, but she also works in countless individual ways that make a difference.

I never realized this more clearly than the other night when my wife and I were having dinner at a local restaurant along with Sue and some friends. Halfway into our meal, a confused and careworn woman was wandering around looking for her purse. When I tried to help her in locating the manager, she defensively pulled away. Sue walked with the woman and talked to her. Her words clearly had a calming effect.

Sue called the center and made arrangements to have the woman spend the night. She then left her dinner, and with the help of another friend, drove the woman to the shelter. She returned in time to watch us all finish our dessert. When we encouraged her to order something more, she simply made a joke that the abbreviated meal fit with her diet plans. We all laughed but took notice of yet another example of individual compassion.

At the end of *It's a Wonderful Life*, George Bailey realizes that he had a pretty wonderful life not because his accomplishments were on a grand scale, but because they were on an individual level that touched the lives of so many. "This is why compassionate thought," the Dalai Lama reminds us, "is so very important for humankind." Sue Adams is that compassionate thought in action, and our community is all the richer for it.

ONE FINAL ACCOUNT COMES, once again, from writer Norman Corwin. This story caught my attention because of its every day significance. It's also a good example of Steve Allen's comment from my first response: "I care much more about the ratings of mankind than about the ratings of my TV show." As this 'moment' demonstrates, the ratings went up a couple of points.

Years ago, while watching a baseball game on TV, I saw Orel Hershiser, pitching for the Dodgers, throw a fastball that hit a batter. The camera was on a close-up of Hershiser, and I could read his lips as he mouthed, "I'm sorry." The batter, taking first base, nodded to the pitcher in a friendly way, and the game went on.

Just two words, and I felt good about Hershiser and the batter and the game all at once. Only a common courtesy, but it made an impression striking enough for me to remember after many a summer.

Look, let's not kid ourselves. It would be foolish to hope that kindness, consideration, and compassion will right wrongs, heal wounds, keep the peace, and set the new millennium on course to recover from inherited ills. That would be asking a lot from even a heaven-sent methodology, and heaven is not in that business. But why linger? Why wait to begin planting seeds, however long they take to germinate? It took us 200-plus years to get into the straits we now occupy, and it may take us long again to get out, but there must be a beginning.

It comes down to the value of exemplars, which can

be either positive or negative, and it works like this: Because of the principle that a calm sea and a prosperous voyage do not make news but a shipwreck does, most circulated news is bad news. The badness of it is publicized, and the negative publicity attracts more of the same through imitation.

But good can be as communicable and catching as evil, and this is where kindness and compassion come into play. So long as conscionable and caring people are around, so long as they are not muted or exiled, so long as they remain alert in thought and action, there is a chance for contagions of the right stuff, whereby democracy becomes no longer a choice of lesser evils, whereby the right to vote is not betrayed by staying away from the polls, whereby the freedoms of speech, assembly, religion, and dissent are never forsaken.

12

what do you stand for?

It STARTED WITH A QUESTION.

I had just finished speaking to a group of businessmen about the need for a greater commitment to ethical standards in our lives. According to the Josephson Institute of Ethics, there have been more ethics scandals in the last five years than in the previous five decades combined.

At the end of the talk, one man raised his hand and asked, "How did we get in this mess?"

"Maybe," I speculated, "we lost our sense of purpose. Maybe we've forgotten what we once stood for." Our idealism, our spirit seemed to be centered in our collective purpose. We were a nation of people who pulled together, supported one another to overcome any obstacle.

"Americanism," Teddy Roosevelt once said, "means the virtues of courage, honor, justice, truth, sincerity and hardihood." Those are strong words, proud words, words that define a country – its people and its purpose. But where is that purpose today? We seem to be more focused on obtaining rock-hard abs than rock-hard ethical standards.

Somewhere in our search for the good life, for our families and ourselves, we compromised. Not all at once, but in little ways and over many years. We fudged the numbers. Not a lot. Just a little bit because we had a deadline to meet. Or we took advantage of information, not for ourselves but perhaps for a worthy organization. We told lies of convenience that we thought wouldn't hurt anybody until slowly, little by little, we justified, rationalized, and compromised what we once stood for.

If Roosevelt's words seemed to define us as a country, the rest of his quote may appear surprisingly prophetic. "The things that will destroy America are prosperity-at-any-price, peace-at-any-price, safety-first instead of duty first, the love of soft living and the get-rich-quick theory of life."

If we are ever going to return to the standards we once had, we're going to have to stop the relentless need to finger-point and blame and begin to take a good look in the mirror and ask ourselves what we stand for.

Then, we need to take action.

First, we need to commit to a set of standards that we know to be right. The Ten Commandments and Golden Rule are a good start, but those standards should also reflect a deep commitment to being both responsible and accountable along with a sincere desire to strive to do our best in all circumstances.

Second, we need to raise our awareness of ethics in the decisions we make on a daily basis: are we treating others honestly, fairly, with respect and consideration? Ben Franklin said, "The noblest question in the world is, what good may I do in it?" Ethics is not about what we say or what we intend. It's about what we *do*. *How* we utilize our principles, in small ways, as well as those that challenge the courage of our convictions, will determine the purpose and course of our lives.

Third, we need to stress competent ethical reasoning. One way is to adopt the decision-making model advocated by the Josephson Institute of Ethics:

1. An ethical decision-maker considers the interests and well-being of all likely to be affected by their actions.

2. An ethical decision-maker makes decisions characterized by their core, ethical principles of Respect, Trustworthiness, Responsibility, Fairness, Citizenship and Caring. These principles always take precedence over non-ethical values – such as hard work, competitiveness, sense of humor.

3. If it is clearly necessary to choose one ethical value over another; the ethical decision-maker will do the thing that he or she sincerely believes to be best for society in the long run.

Finally, we need to cultivate a culture of cooperation. We need to focus less on rights and more on the responsibilities we have to each other. So many times people fail to consider the effect their decisions have on others. In an interview about the 1996 Everest tragedy, climber Jon Krakauer observed, "...we were a bunch of individuals who liked each other...and got along well enough, but we never had this feeling that we were all in it together. ...We were all in it for ourselves when we should have been in it for each other."

But we can change that. And that change begins when we are willing to stand up and stand *for* our highest aspirations.

Does this sound unrealistic – too idealistic?

After speaking to a group of executives from a large retail industry, I was approached by the president of one company who said, "Sitting out there listening to you, I was wondering – is this guy living in the real world? Does he have any clue about the competitive pressures we face? Then I thought, what if I caught one of my own people fudging the numbers, deceiving me about our business in order to meet a goal? That's when I realized how important my example and the example set forth by my managers is to our long-term success."

I'm not saying this is easy. Good character is formed by living under conditions that demand good conduct. But let's try this –

Let's *try* working with others in a truly cooperative way.

Let's take responsibility more seriously than we take ourselves.

Let's recognize that we can be honest and fair and still be tough.

Let's criticize less and inspire more.

Let's encourage leadership more than salesmanship.

Let's pursue a reputation for honor more than we honor elevating the bottom line.

Let's strive to become a little more heroic in our own lives instead of looking to others.

Let's demonstrate the courage of our convictions instead of giving in to the expediency of short-term gains.

And let's realize that we may be able to negotiate many

things, but we will never negotiate our integrity.

We can achieve all these things *and* get the job done, if we think before we act – treat others as we want to be treated.

We can, if we consider that it's okay to be skeptical, but destructive to be relentlessly cynical. Cynicism damages the long-term ideal that we can always be better than we are.

We can, if we remember that we are all in this together and that "This country," as Teddy Roosevelt reminds us, "will not be a good place for *any* of us to live in, unless we make it a good place for *all* of us to live in."

We can, if we embrace compassion, not when it's used as part of a catchphrase, but as the universal truth that it is and the individual value of seeing ourselves in another that is so critical to our progress.

And when we get tired and feel swallowed-up by the endless details of our lives, believing that nothing we do will ever make a difference, we need to consider Mother Teresa's reminder that, "We are not called to do great things, only little things with great love."

A RECENT VISIT TO NEW YORK found me, once again, at the Metropolitan Museum of Art staring at *The Death of Socrates*. This time, I was drawn to the great philosopher's face and expression. Ready to drink the hemlock, left arm raised, he's making one final philosophical point. What is he saying? In the last moments of his life, how might he respond to my question?

"The greatest way to live with honor is to be what we pretend to be."

acknowledgements

PEOPLE KNOW PEOPLE, and good luck trying to get something done when you don't know the *right* people.

Simply put, without these people my job would have been difficult…a *lot* more difficult–

Jeremy Adams, Sue Adams, Bill Allen, Pam Baucom, Pat Boeckenstedt, Millie Bonacci, Bob Bostock, Sam Broadnax, Amanda Butler, Vince Cancro, Peggy Corcoran, Nina Courtney, Sonny Courtney, Leslie Devlin, Dr. Freddye Davy, James Dodson, Sue Fellows, Lynn Fox, Matt Hanser, David Hochberg, Jesse Huot, Bradley James, Deborah Jones, Diane Kinderwater, (The Venerable) Lhakdor, Jamie O'Boyle, John Owens, Denise Perry, Kay Pettijohn, Mary Porcelli, Kerstin Sachl, Randy Schultz, Virginia Schultz, Jason Spitz, Bernard Spigner, Ray Stallone, Dave Steward, Fran Striker, Jr., Barbara Sweeny, Peggy Veljkovic, Kathy Walburn and Russ Williams.

Special appreciation to Dr. Howard Cutler, psychiatrist and co-author with the Dalai Lama on *The Art of Happiness*. Howard started out as a contributor, later a friend. To his great credit, Howard shared his experience and made me feel less alone in my pursuits.

Michael Josephson – my own Socrates – who put me on the path.

The two Lauras: Tennen and Tucker – for their insight and support. Their questions and comments helped me become clearer and more cogent.

Harry Sims, who did more than keep my participles from dangling.

Norman Corwin for his special wisdom and counsel on persistence as well as the most effective choice of words to drive the point home.

Caren Rager, indefatigable transcribe.

And finally, to Bob Shreve whose introductory story began it all.

Thanks, everyone!

your turn

In THE TALKS I GIVE to groups around the country, the one thing I find people looking for are stories of people who do it right, who act out of a set of ethical principles. I think we all have a need to be reminded and inspired to be our best.

If you, or someone you know, has an interesting story relating to any of the ethical values discussed in this book, here's your chance to respond to the same questionnaire I sent in the first go-round:

- What do you stand for – what principle(s) have you lived by?
- Describe a 'moment of principle' in which your convictions were tested or a story in which you were inspired by another.

Send your responses to:
What Do You Stand For?
PO Box 41759
Santa Barbara, CA 93140

about the author

JIM LICHTMAN has been writing and speaking on ethics to corporations, associations and schools since 1995. His Op-ed pieces have appeared in *The Minneapolis Star Tribune, Houston Chronicle, Philadelphia Inquirer, Chicago Tribune,* and *New York Times.*

The Washington Post called Jim's first book, *The Lone Ranger's Code of the West – An Action-Packed Adventure in Values and Ethics,* "…entertaining and informative." *New York Daily News* columnist Stanley Crouch called it, "…an attempt to ring the bells of ethics and courage once more."

For more information, go to: www.scribblers-ink.com

about the type

ITC BERKELEY OLDSTYLE is a Tony Stan redrawing of Frederic Goudy's original Californian typeface, created in 1938 for the University of California Press in Berkeley. Berkeley Oldstyle contains much of Goudy's original Californian design and adds features of other Goudy typefaces such as Kennerley, Goudy Oldstyle, Deepdene and Booklet Oldstyle. Characterized by its calligraphic elegance and subtlety, ITC Berkeley Oldstyle is easy to read and pleasurable to the eye.